MW00831618

THE STORY OF THE
PLOTT HOUND

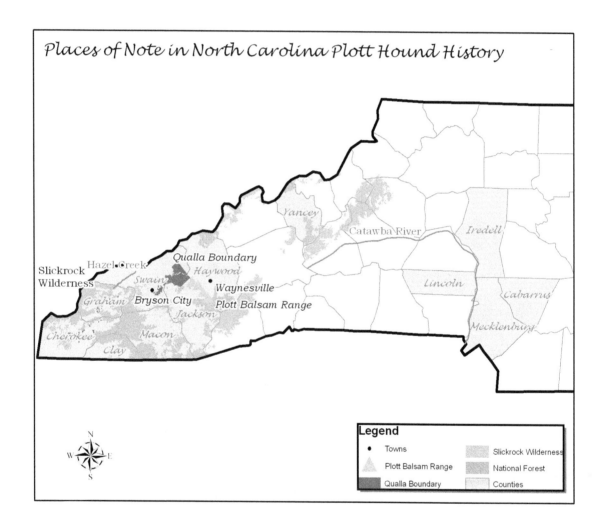

Places of Note in North Carolina Plott Hound History

Hazel Creek
Slickrock Wilderness
Qualla Boundary
Haywood
Swain
Waynesville
Bryson City
Plott Balsam Range
Graham
Jackson
Cherokee
Macon
Clay
Yancey
Catawba River
Iredell
Lincoln
Cabarrus
Mecklenburg

Legend
• Towns
▲ Plott Balsam Range
Qualla Boundary
Slickrock Wilderness
National Forest
Counties

N
W E
S

THE STORY OF THE
PLOTT HOUND

Bob Plott

THE
History
PRESS

Published by The History Press
Charleston, SC 29403
www.historypress.net

Front cover art: *Strike and Stay*, watercolor, 10 x 14 inches.
By Elizabeth Ellison. www.elizabethellisonwatercolors.com

Unless otherwise noted, all images courtesy of Frank Methven, John R. Jackson, Bob Plott and Plott family archives.

First published 2007
Second printing 2009
Third printing 2010
Fourth printing 2012
Fifth printing 2012
Sixth printing 2012

ISBN 9781540217684

Library of Congress Cataloging-in-Publication Data

Plott, Robert.
The story of the Plott hound : strike and stay / Robert Plott.
p. cm.
Includes bibliographical references.

1. Plott hound. I. Title.
SF429.P66P56 2007
636.753'6--dc22
2007041049

Notice: The information in this book is true and complete to the best of our knowledge. It is offered without guarantee on the part of the author or The History Press. The author and The History Press disclaim all liability in connection with the use of this book.

This book is dedicated to the joy of my life, my son, Jacob Morgan Plott. My hope is that someday he will share the story of our family and our dogs with his children and grandchildren.

The bear got in a hole. The dogs charged in one after another. They got beat up pretty bad, but they stayed at it, and charged until they got him. If a dog would not stay all day, my daddy killed them. He had to stay and fight, he had to stay with the bear at the tree. This breed of dog won't quit, he may get clawed and chewed, but he will be back next week. It is one with plenty of gut. The man who isn't game isn't fit to have him.

—"Big" George Plott
describing the Plott family bear hounds to author Michael Frome in the early 1960s

One thing you could always count on with a "Von" Plott–bred Plott hound, was that it would strike a bear trail and stay on it. And stay and stay and stay. There was just no quit in his dogs.

—C.E. "Bud" Lyon
describing the Plott hounds of H.V. "Von" Plott to Bob Plott in 2007

CONTENTS

FOREWORD

An interesting pecularity of modern-day bear hunters—something that most would never expect—is an insatiable hunger for things relating to the sport's past. Granted, much has changed, and in some respects, hunting bear with hounds has undergone a revolution. Advancements in telemetry and communication, transportation and firearm technology have brought significant progress to one of the nation's most demanding and impressive pastimes. Yet, in other ways, things have essentially stayed much the same. For thousands of modern-day houndsmen, the thrill of the chase continues to be a siren call, as it was almost two centuries ago; and despite the use of modern accoutrements, the basic methodology—striking, running, baying and treeing—remains unaltered. With this in mind, one might convincingly argue that among those things best bonding past with present, at least for bear hunting sportsmen, is an inordinate attraction to the history and tradition of their favorite outdoor activity. This is especially the case with those who hunt and promote America's premier big game dog, the Plott hound.

It is not difficult to understand the Plott owner's captivation with their dog's past. Of all America's scent-hound breeds, the Plott remains unchallenged in terms of its rich and varied legacy. The fame of the Brooke hounds of colonial aristocracy; the so-called Irish importations; the redoubtable Birdsongs, Triggs and Walkers; the fleet of foot July hounds, Goodmans; and Sugar Loafs is minor in comparison. As one historian in describing the Plott breed maintains, "Their exploits are legion, and the years have shaped them into legend." Here is Americana at its best—an "Old Yeller"–type dog casting long and indelible shadows on the folklore, history and fabric of Appalachian society.

Not many years ago, North Carolina recognized the Plott breed as the "Official State Dog." If ever there was a more likely candidate for national honors, it would be hard pressed to surpass the lasting imprint, both historical and otherwise, of the Plott's brindle bear dogs.

On more than one occasion, various authors and columnists have sought to tell at least some of the Plott story. As long ago as 1905, when Arthur F. McFarlane penned *Outing*

Magazine's "The Last of the Breed of Plott" and Horace Kephart's "Compass Trees, Feathered Worms, and Mudchucks" appeared in *Field and Stream*, writers have tried to better acquaint the public with the Plott bear hound.

Without question, however, the most factual and entertaining treatment of the Plott was found in Kephart's *Our Southern Highlanders*, a monumental effort, first published in 1913, which continues to provide the best primary account of the early breed. Following this pioneering work were numerous articles and columns penned by others in publications such as the *New York Times*, *Outdoor Life* and *Sports Afield*.

Recently, more conspicuous scholarship has arrived. David M. Duffey's *Hunting Hounds* (1972), for instance, was perhaps the first in-depth, concentrated study of American scent and sight hounds. Then as late as 2002 Dr. Andreas F. Von Recum completed another work, *Hunting with Hounds*, which like Duffey's earlier effort dealt with American scent and coursing breeds. Both spoke of brindle bear dogs at length, yet a single volume dedicated solely to the study of the Plott has failed to appear—that is until Bob Plott's *The Story of the Plott Hound—Strike & Stay*.

Strike & Stay has been a labor of love fueled by an intense, though bridled, pride in family, plus a fervent desire to learn more about the dog. For Bob, this has been no easy task. Fact often had to be sifted from fiction: decades of propoganda often blurred the line. And, when dealing with a subject so enmeshed in folklore, if not legend, it was sometimes difficult for even him to be objective. Bob, however, diligently forged ahead to produce a title that includes both scholarly and commercial appeal. For the veteran houndsman and those who have cultivated the Plott for years, *Strike & Stay* deals with familiar and interesting subjects. For the neophyte, however, his work is a boon, an account of America's most colorful and extraordinary hunting dog. Indeed an enjoyable introduction to the world of the big game hound, and a course in Plottology 101. Perhaps more importantly, it provides excellent groundwork for another more concentrated, extensive study of the subject in the future.

—John R. Jackson

Author's note: John Jackson is a past president of the American Plott Association and is a charter member of the group. He is a member and officer of the North Carolina Bearhunters Association and the National Plott Hound Association. He is a longtime columnist for *Full Cry* magazine and was the 2006 winner of the prestigous Frank Methven Big Game Award. Jackson is widely recognized as the eminent historian on the Plott hound breed and he is an accomplished bear and hog hunter. He is a retired educator and now serves as pastor to several churches. Jackson proudly carries on the legacy of the Taylor Crockett Plott hound at his Little Elk Kennels, near Boone, North Carolina.

ACKNOWLEDGEMENTS

Over the years many folks have encouraged me to write a book. But none more often than my friends Matt Mull, the late Bud Lewin, Lynn and Ann Moretz, George and Elizabeth Ellison, Billy Chapman, Mike Pritchard, Bill Carter and my wife Janice Plott. I thank them all for their support and encouragement.

But of that group, George and Elizabeth Ellison deserve special thanks. George not only helped me find a publisher, but more importantly, he gave me the confidence to write. By serving as my mentor, and editor, George patiently, and free of charge, provided me an education that few will find in the best universities. In addition, he aided me in making many great contacts who played an integral role in my research. If this book is good, George deserves a lot of credit for it. If it is not, it is all on me. George is one of my heroes and I am forever in his debt.

Thanks also to Elizabeth Ellison for the magnificent painting of a Plott hound that she did for the cover of this book. She is the consumate artist.

More than one hundred people were interviewed for this book, and I wish I could have interviewed a hundred more. I gratefully thank them all. But none was more important than Plott hound expert John R. Jackson. John was an absolutely invaluable and objective resource on all things related to the Plott family and the Plott hound breed. But just as importantly, as the foremost expert of the Plott breed and a fine writer in his own right, he proofed the work for historical and factual errors. This book has been a blessing to me in so many ways, but perhaps the best of all the blessings was meeting and becoming friends with John. I look up to John the same way he looked up to his friend and mentor, the late Taylor Crockett.

Other Plott hound experts, like Steve Fielder, Roy Stiles, APA President Rodney Burris, NPHA President Joe Polly, Jason Bickford, Randy Wolfe and John Hagin, all offered invaluable assistance to this project, as did Todd King of the North Carolina Bear Hunters Association. And living legends of Plott hound history, such as Sam George, Robert Jones and C.E. "Bud" Lyon, were all extremely generous in offering their assistance. I am especially grateful to Bud for his friendship and for the fine pup he gave my son. Another Plott dog living legend, Frank Methven, also provided wonderful information, insight and many pictures for this project. I am honored and priveleged to have him as a friend and mentor.

Mark A. Baker was another superb writing coach in this process, and I thank him, as well as Charles S. Brown and Michael Alton, for not only their expert insight on life in the eighteenth century, but more importantly for their treasured friendship and support.

Jim Campbell provided wonderfully detailed genalogical research on the Plott family, as did my cousins Jeff Crisp and Mark Faust.

Daniel Whitener, Clay Ludlam and Joe Barker brought me into the twenty-first century with their computer expertise and invaluable advice. Thanks for your help and patience. Thanks to Katy Talbert for the author photo. You did a good job with not much to work with.

Several individuals and publications were extremely helpful in both opening their archives to me and in providing back issues for research. They are: Ann Moore of the Foxfire Foundation, Tanya M. Raab and Vicki Rand of *UKC Bloodlines Magazine*, Diana Rupp of *Sports Afield* magazine and Greg Jenkins and Gloria Smith of *Wildlife in North Carolina* magazine.

Bill Gibson and Ryan Sherby offered valuable insight on the southern mountain region, provided me with excellent contacts and also did the map work for the book. George Frizzell, head of special collections for the Hunter Library at Western Carolina University, not only opened his archives to me, but also took the time to print out and provide many valuable books and online resources for me.

Without the patience and support of my wife Janice, and our son Jacob, this project would never have happened. Thanks also to the best parents in the world, the late P.G. "Shine" Plott and my mom Mary, for making me a Plott. Money can't buy that.

Finally, thanks to Lee Handford and the folks at The History Press for their patience with a first-time writer, and for making a dream come true.

INTRODUCTION

Like a lot of folks in the United States, my ancestors left Europe a long time ago in hopes of finding a better life in America. In our case we left from Germany and the year was 1750. And like most of these people, my relatives, the Plott brothers, literally risked their lives in embarking on their adventure to a new world.

But unlike these other immigrants, the Plotts are one of the few families that can say they risked their lives to get their *dogs* to their new home. Other people also brought dogs to the new world. But few, if any of them, aside from the Plotts, can lay claim to not only bringing their hounds to America, but also creating a whole new special breed of dog. Equally impressive is how they managed to inspire a long lasting, fierce devotion among their descendants, friends and supporters, to preserve, improve and perpetuate the legacy of their very extraordinary breed of dog—the Plott bear hound.

As Plott historian John Jackson once told me, "The story of the Plott family and their dogs is one of pure Americana." Jackson's assessment is absolutely correct. Like much of American history, it is a story of triumph and tragedy and of joy and sadness. But most of all, it is a story of a tenacious dedication to the preservation of a noble breed of animal by their proud owners. Moreover, it is a story of the magnificent Plott hound itself—an animal that has not only managed to survive, but has thrived in the United States for more than two centuries.

But the story of the Plott hound is just that—a story. A story that is equal parts fact and legend. Some of the story is easily authenticated, but much of it is not. I verified as many historical facts as possible regarding the history of the breed. As a Plott family member I have also included stories that are oral history or family tradition, as well as stories from current and past legends of Plott hound history. These stories are supposedly true, though in some cases there is little documentation to verify them.

In still other cases where stories or facts greatly differed, I either omitted them entirely or consulted the most reputable sources available and included their versions. But in doing so I have tried to point out that they may only be educated opinion or speculation.

However, there are also stories that I included that probably are just tall tales. I included them simply because I felt they were both entertaining, yet made a good point. I think a majority of readers can easily identify these stories, but in most instances I still noted that they might be questionable.

Nevertheless, I am sure that there are those who will take issue with some aspects of this book and they are certainly entitled to their opinion. Plott hound people are passionate about their dogs and the origins of their dogs, as well as who has the best hounds or who has done the most for the breed. I totally understand that and I respect them for it. But I hope that they can appreciate and respect my passion for the breed too. After all, it is my family and our dogs that we are discussing. But I want to make it clear that I do *not* claim to be the foremost historian, expert or writer regarding the subject of Plott hounds. Nor do I claim to be the world's best bear hunter. I most certainly am not.

But I do know the subject. And, as someone who has not only researched it, but has grown up immersed in the Plott hound legend, I feel more than qualified to write about it.

The history of the Plott hound is a great story and one that needs to be told. I hope that this book not only fairly tells the story of the breed and those who support it, but that it will also inspire further books on the subject. Perhaps esteemed Plott historian John Jackson will write further on this topic. I certainly hope that he does.

But until then, I think this is a good start. I hope I did justice to this great story and that you will enjoy reading the story as much as I did researching and writing it. It is also my desire that perhaps the book will instill a spark of interest in the reader to do their own research and get involved with Plott hounds. You will be glad you did.

Chapter One

THE GAMEKEEPER

Elias Isaac Plott was tired and worried. Working in the Black Forest as a gamekeeper in all seasons, for years on end, had drained his stamina and weakened his spirit. The fatigue from his work seemed never ending, but this paled in comparison to his enormous emotional burdens. Plott was worried about his two teenage sons and what the future held for them. As a professional hunter he understood better than most his own mortality, but worse yet, realized the lack of future opportunities for his sons in a land seeped in centuries of feudalism.

It was the spring of 1750, but the warmth of the planting season had not yet come to his Rhenish Palatinate Valley. The ache of one too many harsh and bitterly cold winters spent out-of-doors lingered deep within his bones. And the long, pleasant days of summer remained but a distant memory. At the age of forty-eight, Plott was no longer a young man, and for a while now had felt old age creeping in, but never more so than that winter.

Without much compensation or relief, Elias for years had guarded the game of the favored dukes or barons near what is now known as Heidelberg, Germany. His job as a gamekeeper required him to be outdoors year-round, and at the beck and call of his employer twenty-four hours a day, seven days a week, no matter what the weather. A gamekeeper's job in the Palatinate was not much more than that of a glorified sharecropper and really not much better than a slave. It was not the profession made glamourous and exciting in classical literature and later in the movies, but was instead a brutally tough and dangerous job, consisting in equal parts of hunter, guide, conservationist, veterinarian, policeman and game warden.

Plott surely saw no future above his own dismal lot for his two sons, Johannes and Enoch. The dust of time has covered the details of the brothers' backgrounds, for some family members say they were twins, while others say Johannes was sixteen and Enoch a year older at seventeen. But regardless of those details, what did the future hold for his sons? To Elias, surely it must have looked grim. Even as much as he loved the outdoors, he must have wanted something better for his sons than the wet feet and frostbitten hands of a gamekeeper, which was probably the best the boys could have hoped for if they stayed in their native land. He lived in a country in turmoil, and he had never known it any other way. It was a country rife with religious persecution, war and poverty, with no real form of central government. A land that was ruled by feudal lords or barons, who for the most part were not much better than the worst sort of dictator.

Was this a place for his sons to marry and raise a family? Plott surely must have thought not, but as a poor man, he did not have a lot of other options to offer them. Basically their choices were to either tough it out in Germany or migrate somewhere else, as thousands of Palatines had already done. Over the previous few decades, starting in the early 1700s, Palatines had moved in droves first to England and later to America. By 1745 there were already 45,000 Palatines in the American colony of Pennsylvania alone. Many of Plott's fellow countrymen had already considered and exercised such a migration to escape the terminal future of their feudal homeland.

Plott perhaps felt that he and his wife were too old to start a new life in a new world and that the boys were young enough to acclimate themselves quickly there. He also probably had heard of the large Swiss-German settlement in New Bern, North Carolina. Elias knew his sons would have plenty of options there or in the numerous other Palatine settlements scattered across the eastern seaboard of America.

Were there relatives or friends in one of these settlements who Elias had already arranged to welcome the boys, offering safe refuge for these young strangers in a strange land? Or were they considering working as either indentured servants or craftsman apprentices to bankroll their start in the new world?

Maybe they had gotten themselves in some sort of trouble and their father wanted them to leave the country for their own safety. After all, stringent social class or caste laws were still strictly enforced by the ruling upper class. A poor man was not allowed to talk to, much less marry, anyone outside his own social class. Perhaps the Plott boys were simply rascals who were run out of town—or maybe they stole the baron's dogs and *had* to run away. Or they could have just been spirited young men looking for adventure who *chose* to run away from home, and knew no one at all in this foreign land. If so, this only makes their journey all the bolder.

No one knows for sure, but as a Plott who grew up hearing the family story of my great-great-great-grandfather Johannes, I always believed that it happened the following way. I think that Elias Plott was simply hoping for a better future for his sons. As a result, I believe he planned for his sons to immigrate to America and did what he could to help them. Since he had little or no money, I think that he gave them a generous parting gift of the only thing of real value that he had access to—his dogs.

Whether or not that is true, we do know that Johannes and Enoch Plott took some of the family's (or the baron's) most valued possessions—five hunting dogs—with them to America in the summer of 1750. Legend has it that two of these hounds were buckskin-colored, and the remaining three were brindled dogs.

And oh, what dogs they were! Even as special as Elias Plott knew those dogs were then, neither he nor his sons could have ever imagined that they would ultimately, over the next two hundred years, become one of the best, if not *the* best, breed of big game hunting dogs the world has even seen—the Plott bear hound.

Chapter Two

GERMAN ORIGINS

Before we follow the boys on their journey to America, we should first take a look at just what made these dogs special enough that the teens chose to take five of them on their transatlantic trek. From my research this was not that common and of itself tells us something of the value of the animals to the Plott family. But just what type or breed of dog were these special animals?

The late Lawrence Plott, a sixth-generation descendant of Johannes Plott, believed that the closest relative to a current-day Plott hound is the Hanoverian *schweisshund*. Lawrence was quoted in an article in *Wildlife in North Carolina* magazine (October 1983) stating that he felt this to be true after having spent fifteen years in Germany during and after World War II, and researching the subject extensively.

Certainly, if you look through any dog journal or encylcopedia, some of the Hanoverian hounds pictured there do indeed look like many of the modern-day Plott hounds. They appear to be a bit smaller and more athletic looking than your typical hound breed, with shorter ears, tighter skin and a brindle coloring, very much like a Plott dog.

John Jackson, a leading expert on the history of the Plott hound and family, agrees that the Hanoverian dog is a close match to the Plott hound. But, he adds that there more than likely were other breeds involved in the original lineage, though no one knows for sure. According to Steve Fielder's fine website, Plottdogs.com, Von and John Plott both told Dale Brandenburger in 1949 that they had no idea from what stock their dogs originated but acknowledged that the Hanoverian dog was probably in the mix. The key words there are "in the mix."

Henry Vaughn "Von" Plott, who was most certainly the best-known hunter and dog breeder of the twentieth-century Plott family, recalled to several *Foxfire* staff members in a 1976 interview that:

> They [the Plott family] *developed the dogs in Germany. I don't know what they tried to get the Plott. I wasn't there. I never been there. They put out good stuff now, the Germans*

are smart people! I don't know what their name for the Plott dog was in German. But when the old man [Johannes] brought them here they named them after him. They called them Plotts. But I don't know what they were. They used the dogs to hunt bear and Russian boar in Germany. So these dogs have been here over two hundred years.

After pausing to reflect a moment, Von continued, "Well, the old man [Johannes] had some idea of what he had, he figured they'd be worth something to him, and they HAVE been worth something to him."

Indeed.

In 1973 Von Plott told a *Sports Afield* magazine writer much the same thing, leading that writer to surmise that the genealogy of the breed "is purely guess work." Von, in 1947, also told writer Jim Gasque in his book *Hunting and Fishing in the Great Smokies* that "they brought with them a pack of bluish brindle hounds that had back of them the blood of the cold-nosed *schweisshund*, a strain of German hound." "*Schweisshund*" literally means bloodhound in German and is a generic German term for bloodhound dogs. Many writers, as Gasque did, and perhaps Von himself, have misused this term as a specific breed name, which is not the case.

Yet, even today most major dog organizations, kennel clubs and publications stick to the simple safe answer that the Plott hound is a direct descendant of the Hanoverian hound and leave it at that, which to some degree is true. I do not, however, believe that to be entirely true, although I do believe that the Hanoverian plays a part, a very big part, in the bloodline. As Lawrence Plott said in 1983 and John Jackson in 2007, the Hanoverian is the closest thing we have that can be compared to the Plott hound of today.

So, while it is indeed probable that the Plott hound has Hanoverian bloodlines, I believe that those aren't the only bloodlines evident, as some dog books and organizations would have us believe. Other breeds also likely played a key part in the makeup of the dog that the Plott brothers took with them to America. To fully understand why I believe this to be true, we must first look at the role of the German gamekeeper, as well as the times and geographical area in which he (in this case Elias Plott, and his sons) lived and worked.

The gamekeeper job or *wildheger*, as it was known in German, was not only difficult and dangerous but also required a wide variety of skills. He not only had to police his employer's property, but he also had to control and destroy unwelcome animal and human predators that could kill or infect his employer's domestic stock. To further complicate the job, the gamekeeper was bound by a strict, ancient honor code that they were all sworn to adhere to. Any kill he made on a hunt must be a quick and clean one, and under no circumstances was a wounded animal ever to be left to run away and die a slow death. There could be no exceptions to this rule.

Regardless of how good the gamekeeper was at all of these skills, even the best needed help to do his job safely and correctly. And, of course, their families, especially their sons, played an integral part in that role. Even so, the most valuable aide to the gamekeeper was his pack of dogs. He simply could not do his job without them.

John Jackson coined the phrase "dual purpose dogs" to describe the early American Plott hounds because they had to be not only hunting dogs, but herding dogs, too. I have expanded on that a bit to describe *both* the early American Plott hound, as well as their European forefathers, as "multipurpose dogs." By this I mean that like their masters, they both had to have multiple skills. They had to be fine hunting hounds, as well as fine farm and herding dogs.

Many dog breeds possess some of these traits or characteristics, yet few possess all of them. Consequently, over many generations the gamekeeper constantly bred his dogs in an effort to get these desired traits. He obviously could not have understood the scientific terms of modern-day genetic breeding, but he certainly understood results. He used the old-time method of breeding the best to the best to get the best, and eventually was able to get the exact dog he needed for the job. This is why I do not believe that these early dogs can be so easily described as any one specific breed, especially when you consider the history and turbulent times of the gamekeeper's homeland and the various dog breeds of the region that he had to work with.

The area where I believe the Plott family and their dogs originated—along the right bank of the Rhine River in the Black Forest—like the rest of the country had been a war-torn area since the times of the Roman empire. In 800 BC the Celts settled near what is now Heidelberg, Germany. They lived and prospered there until they were driven out by the Alemanic tribe in AD 260. The Celts had a close relationship with the people already living there whom they called *"Germani,"* from which the word German was derived.

The Celts themselves loved to hunt and found kindred spirits in their *Germani* neighbors, whom they described as having little patience for organized agriculture. Like the *Germani*, the Celts loved their hunting dogs and considered the breeding of them to be an art form. They used dogs similar to Irish wolfhounds as war dogs in battle and utilized their breeding skills to develop several varieties of this breed, including setters, terriers and water spaniels.

So, it is clearly evident that dating back to ancient times there were already multipurpose dogs of sorts in the Black Forest area. But there were other outside influences, too. To the west of Germany is France, another country that would wage war on and invade the region in the 1600s. To the south is Switzerland, to the north Belgium and to the southeast Austria, all countries that through war or trade brought dogs into this area. Let's look at some of the other dog breeds known to be in Germany that were probably familiar to the Plott family by the early 1700s.

Of course, we must start with the old standby, the Hanoverian hound. This breed dates back to the Middle Ages and has direct ties to the seventeenth-century French Saint Hubert hound, as well as to both Belgium and Switzerland. The United Kennel Club's description of a modern-day Plott hound is nearly identical to some strains of the Hanoverian. These dogs, like the Plotts, are known for their superb tracking skills; keen, cold nose; and good disposition. This hound certainly has a lot of what we recognize today as "Plott traits," and it is surely a very big part of what I call "the mix."

The Tyrolean hound, or *Tyroler bracke*, descends directly from the previously discussed Celtic dogs. It can be documented as far back as 1500 and originated in Austria. It is smaller than the Hanoverian, weighing only forty to fifty pounds and standing sixteen to twenty inches tall. Its ears and head are similar to the Hanoverian, with the same round, dark brown eyes. But the body is longer and legs shorter, with thick, close cropped hair and a variety of coat colors. These colors range from black-and-tan and fawn tricolor to a red-yellow black-and-tan. White markings are common on the chest, collar, legs and feet. The Tyrolean hound's tail is carried high and is thick, dense and long. The Tyrolean, with its distinctive white markings—like those of some early Plott hounds—and its Hanoverian-like head and ears with similar tracking abilities, does indeed possess some early Plott dog characteristics. The breed's love for the hunt, combined with its ability to relate well to people, make it another possibility to add to the early Plott hound "mix."

The German hound, or *Deutsche bracke*, is another canine breed known to have been in the region at that time. It also should be considered for our Plott hound ancestry list. This dog dates back to ancient Celtic times, and like the name implies, originated in Germany. It is a smaller dog, standing only fifteen to seventeen inches high and weighing from forty to forty-five pounds, and it has medium-sized, dark brown eyes. The *Deutsche* is characterized by its broad chest, muscular body, superb hunting skills and Hanoverian-like head. In these areas, the *Deutsche* perfectly fits the Plott hound profile.

Another hound of the region that fits the same profile is the Austrian *brandlbracke*, which descends directly from the ancient Celtic hounds. Like the Plott, the *brandlbracke* has a sturdy body and high-set, smooth ears, and they are renowned hunting dogs.

The lesser-known *steiri rauhhaarbracke* is another Austrian dog of Celtic ancestry, and it looks much like the other Austrian and German hounds mentioned, except for its solid pale yellow or reddish yellow color. If it is indeed part of the "mix," this could possibly explain the buckskin-colored Plotts that the boys took with them to America.

The German shorthair and German boxer are also worthy of consideration and were available for the Plott's eighteenth-century breeding pool. I find the German shorthair to be particularly interesting in that it has many of the same physical characteristics as the Plott dogs. It is well known for its loyalty to its owner and for being a multipurpose hunting dog.

Another intriguing breed is the German Weimaraner. This ancient but commonly known breed perhaps originated in France, but it gained prominence in Germany. None of these more commonly known dogs has the trailing or scent-hound abilities of the breeds previously discussed. But other characteristics do match, such as its athletic and muscular body, short hair, loyalty and fierce protective nature.

Interestingly enough, the German edition of the online encyclopedia *Wikipedia* specifically states in the entry on Plott hounds that the dog is a simple mix of Weimaraner and Hanoverian breeds! Yet their American edition sticks to the common Hanoverian ancestry definition. If this Weimaraner-Hanoverian mix could be conclusively proven or verified, it would be groundbreaking information and finally answer the question of breed origination that Plott dog people have debated for years. However, it must be duly noted that *Wikipedia*, while a valuable resource, is not one without fault. Only about 85 percent of its entries have proven to be entirely accurate, and most, if not all, are submitted by volunteer researchers, who may not be the most scholarly or objective of information sources. Nevertheless, these are still interesting and thought-provoking points, and more study is needed to clarify them.

I have not been able to verify this for sure, but Randy Wolfe of Fountain City, Indiana, a fine dog breeder and hunter himself, says that he was told that a German organization known as the German Hunting Dog Society had also made the Weimaraner-Hanoverian mix claim.

The late John Parris, in a story on the Plott hound in his book *These Storied Mountains* (1972), also suggests that the breed may have Weimaraner blood in "the mix." I have also heard, but to date have not been able to confirm, that another German group, the Association for Black Forest Welding Dogs and Plott Hound Association, contends that the five dogs that Johannes and Enoch Plott took with them on their trip to America were three brindle dogs with total Hanoverian bloodlines and that the two buckskin dogs were in fact full-blooded Weimaraners. (*Welding* means bleeding in German as it relates specifically to bloodhounds.) Hopefully, future research will either verify or dispel this theory.

According to legend, the Plott family had been refining its breeding techniques for many generations by the time the Plott boys and their dogs left Germany for America in 1750. As a result of this, the dogs they took with them possibly contained trace elements of some or all of the mentioned stock, plus some that we do not know about. That is what I believe Von Plott meant when he used the term "in the mix." No one knows for sure exactly what that mix was. But it almost surely was a mix. It definitely was not a full-blooded anything and probably not even a simple fifty-fifty mix. I do want to add again though, that if we were to narrow it down to one breed, the Hanoverian is indeed the closest individual breed to the Plott hound we know today. But I still maintain that the Hanoverian was only a part, albeit a big part, of "the mix," not the entire breed.

I also am not saying that the early Plott was a mix of *all* these breeds, only that they were available for the family to breed and that they possess some traits of the dog we know today as the Plott hound—some more than others. It is also important to remember that expert breeders over many generations can refine breeds to include as little as one-sixty-fourth of a specific bloodline, thus allowing for many different types of breed infusion. Just as importantly, that small one-sixty-fourth part of the bloodline could still possess the dominant gene that defines some major characteristics or traits of the dog. In other words, while a Plott hound's lineage, or any dog's lineage for that matter, may possess only one-sixty-fourth of another breed in its bloodline, that small part may nevertheless play a defining role in what the dog looks like and how it performs.

Clearly the Plott family had the specific need for a multipurpose dog. They also possessed the advanced breeding skills needed to achieve their desired results. Those two factors, combined with the many fine types of dogs available to them in eighteenth-century Germany, lead me to conclude that the original Plott hound was a mix of the best elements of several different dog breeds. Which specific ones, we will probably never know for sure, but we certainly cannot argue with the end results.

Chapter Three

AMERICA

While we will probably never know the specific reasons the Plott boys left home, or exactly what type of dogs they took with them, we do know for sure that Johannes and Enoch Plott, with five prized hounds, left their home and journeyed up the Rhine River to Rotterdam, Holland, around July 1750. There, it is generally believed that they booked passage on the ship *Priscilla*, along with 209 other immigrants from their homeland.

I have often thought what incredible courage this must have taken for two teenage boys to embark on such an adventure. And while I know times and people were different then, I am nevertheless amazed by it. Granted, I am biased, as Johannes is my great-great-great-grandfather, but regardless of the family connection, I can only imagine how scared these boys had to have been leaving their parents and home, going to a new world all alone. It must have been extremely hard on them.

Unfortunately, it would only get harder. Things took a terribly tragic turn when Enoch became sick en route and died. He was buried at sea. Now Johannes was forced to endure not only the death of his only close relative (possibly his twin), but he also had to continue the trip alone, except for his dogs. Surely this sad incident only made him appreciate his hounds even more, as they were the only tie that remained to his family and home.

On September 12, 1750, the *Priscilla* landed in Philadelphia, Pennsylvania. Family tradition has it that Johannes and his dogs then immediately headed south, down the eastern seaboard, to the Swiss-German settlement of New Bern, North Carolina. There is no way to know this for sure, as there is no written record of his whereabouts in America from the time of his arrival in Philadelphia in 1750 until 1759. During those nine years, he may have, as legend has it, proceeded directly to New Bern, North Carolina. Perhaps the baron who employed his family in Germany, or one of his business associates, sent the Plott boys and their hounds to New Bern to serve specifically as station hunters for the town. Historian Harriette Arnow states in her book *Seedtime on the Cumberland* that New Bern was known to have had problems keeping fresh meat in supply for its citizens. She also notes that there were bear hunting dogs there, saying:

"Some had dogs trained to follow bear by scent and then snap and bark at him til he trees." Arnow does not elaborate further on the topic, but it is nonetheless an intriguing possibility to consider.

But Johannes may have instead stayed in the Pennsylvania area or even somewhere else along the way for that matter. We also know nothing regarding his dogs during this time period, though Plott family oral history indicates that the pack had flourished and grown in their new home during this time.

Mystery enshrouds those nine missing years. Some say that Johannes changed his first name to George or Jonathan. Some say that his original surname was Platz and that it, too, was changed to Plott. But later land grant records, as well as his last will and testament filed in Lincoln County, North Carolina, in 1809, indicate that his legal name was George Plott, though it was probably changed from Johannes to George after his arrival in America.

We do not know how Johannes supported himself during this time. Perhaps he hired himself out as a laborer or was indentured to learn a trade or served as an apprentice. Maybe he did indeed work at New Bern or other settlements as a station hunter, using his dogs and woodsman skills to provide game for the settlers. The truth is we just do not know for sure. There is even a rumor that he married during this time, perhaps to a woman with the first name of Lucretia. Another rumor is that the Plott boys were in trouble, and in an effort to leave Germany as quickly as possible they booked cheap passage on a slave ship and were never on the *Priscilla* at all. But again, there is no documentation to support any of this.

The next written record of Johannes (George) Plott occurs in 1759, when he received a land grant in the Granville district of Bute County, North Carolina. This area is now known as Warren County. The Moravian missonary Bishop Augustus Gottlieb Spangenburg, in 1752, was commissioned by his church to find ideal land for settlement in North Carolina. While in this area, he described it in his diary as "not particularly good, yet we are told that it has all been taken up." He added, "One can ride for three hours without seeing anything but pine barrens" and reported that the few farms there were mainly growing corn and raising hogs.

Maybe Johannes had one of those farms or hunted in the pine barrens, maybe not. But this land evidently did not suit him. He moved farther inland in about 1760. This is where we next have record of him in what is now Cabarrus County, North Carolina. It was here that Plott built a farm bordered by Big and Little Coldwater Creeks. Spangenburg had also visited near this area along the Catawba River eight years earlier, and he noted: "There are many hunters here who work little, live like Indians, shoot many deer and sell their skins."

Spangenburg described the rolling hills and beauty of the region, but he reminded his readers that this was still a dangerous place to live. Johannes surely must have found the terrain more to his liking with its abundance of game and lush, thickly forested rolling hills, similar to his Black Forest homeland.

Mecklenburg County, North Carolina court records indicate that in 1762 George (Johannes) Plott married Margret Ann Littleton. They had at least eight children, three of whom were boys. The oldest was John, born in Cabarrus County in 1768, and Henry and Elias were also born there in 1770 and 1784 respectively. Shortly after the birth of Elias, the family moved farther west across the Catawba River into what is now Lincoln County, North Carolina. From here the record again gets a bit confusing.

Though there is no written documentation, oral family history indicates that his dogs had prospered much like his family during that time. It is also believed that they were being used by the Plott family as the multipurpose dogs described in Chapter Two. According to Von Plott, even back then Johannes was tight-lipped as to the background of his dogs, and very careful to ensure that their lineage was kept as pure as possible.

In his 1983 *Wildlife in North Carolina* article, Curtis Wooten suggests that Johannes passed the hounds to his son John in 1780 and that John took them west in 1800 to Haywood County. Upon his arrival there, he supposedly negotiated with Junaluska, the legendary Cherokee chief, for ownership rights to the Balsam Mountain range. Wooten adds that John Plott later settled his family there, in the area now known as Plott Valley. However, this story, too, is incorrect, as John would have been only twelve years old in 1780, and there is no documentation that he ever moved to Haywood County at all. In fact, it appears that John spent most, if not all, of his adult life in or around Cabarrus County, North Carolina, as did his brother Elias.

Furthermore, while the Plott family probably did indeed negotiate with their Cherokee neighbors for rights to their land, it almost certainly would have been Chief Yonaguska, not Junaluska, with whom they negotiated. Junaluska would have been a very young man, only about twenty years old when the Plott family arrived, while Yonaguska would have already been a well-respected chief, at least thirty years old in 1800. Yonaguska's clan lived nearby on Soco Creek, and although a staunch tribal traditionalist, he was well known for being friendly with white settlers.

A more recent article about the Plott dog from *Our State Magazine* (October 2006), written by Janet Pittard, states that Johannes turned over his pack of dogs to Henry Plott in 1780 and moved the family west to the Great Smokies region shortly before that. This too is incorrect, as Henry would have been only ten years old in 1780 and did not move to the Smokies himself until the late 1700s. It is also highly unlikely that Johannes moved the entire family there either, but if he did, it certainly was not before 1780.

Plott historian John Jackson maintains that Johannes Plott never moved or lived in Haywood County at all. He certainly may have visited there, but records show that after moving to Lincoln County, North Carolina, in about 1784, he lived there for the remainder of his life on his farm on Maiden Creek. Furthermore, his will, written in 1809 (and on file in the Lincoln County Courthouse, listing sons Elias and John as executors) further substantiates this fact. It is interesting to note that Johannes signed his name as "gPlott" in his will. But the passenger list of the *Priscilla* shows his signature as Johannes, written in bold, flowing script. So assuming that the list is legitimate, and that Johannes and George were one and the same person, then he was capable of writing his name and perhaps was literate. However, the key points here are that Johannes was still living in Lincoln County, North Carolina, in 1809 when his will was written, and probably had been there for almost twenty-five years. More importantly, he apparently never lived in Haywood County at all.

We should also mention again that, outside of the passenger list of the *Priscilla*, all official documentation regarding Johannes Plott in North Carolina indicates that he was George Plott. Land grant records in Warren, Cabarrus and Lincoln Counties, marriage records in Mecklenburg County and his will in Lincoln County all record him as George, not Johannes, Plott. This may be nothing more than a German name anglicized to English, which was common, but the truth is that there is no official record or documentation of a Johannes Plott being in North Carolina. I personally believe that they are one and the same individual and that Johannes simply changed his name to George. But for the sake of strict historical accuracy this should be duly noted.

Johannes "George" Plott died on his Lincoln County farm in 1810 at the age of seventy-six. He left a rich and long lasting legacy of family and dogs that endures even today. But how did the Plott family and hounds end up in the mountains of Haywood County, North Carolina? The best explanation—and one that most family members have believed to be true—is that Johannes's son Henry was responsible for the start of the Plott hound legend in the Great Smoky Mountains of North Carolina.

Henry Plott married Lydia Osborne in November 1796, and shortly afterward formed a business partnership with her brother Jonathan Osborne. Jonathan and Henry then decided to move west to what was then known as Buncombe County, but is now Haywood County. They would become some of the first white settlers west of the Pigeon River near what is now Canton, North Carolina. This area was still the frontier then, and the men left their families back in the Piedmont while they attempted to carve out a new home for them in the mountains. Family tradition has it that Henry took some, but probably not all, of the Plott family dog pack with him to this beautiful, remote and dangerous area. The men planted their first crops, but they had bad luck as the crops failed due to bad weather and other obstacles. This resulted in the decision to dissolve their partnership. As winter approached, Jonathan Osborne headed back home to his family, but Henry decided to stay and try to make a go of it alone.

It was worse than even a hardy frontiersman like Henry Plott could have ever expected. The mountain winters were incredibly harsh, but he toughed it out and survived the season. Thanks to his fine hounds, he had plenty to eat and was protected from both human and animal predators. Though Johannes and his sons had used their Plott dogs for big game hunting since their arrival in America, it was here, with Henry, that they probably got their first taste of mountain bear hunting.

After surviving that first hard winter, Henry knew he had found the place where he wanted to raise his family. He soon took a state land grant farther west on the waters of Richland and Dick's Creeks. Most experts believe that he moved his family there in about 1799 or 1800. Census records, however, show that Henry was still living in Cabarrus County in 1800. This could be true, but old census records have proven to be notoriously inaccurate, and this could be yet another example of that. Or it could simply reflect that his family was still living in Cabarrus County at the time, while Henry endured his first winter alone in the mountains. If Plott family lore is true, then Henry was indeed here negotiating land rights with the Cherokees in about 1800. But either way, by no later than 1801, Henry Plott, his family and his dogs were firmly established in Haywood County.

The name Dick's Creek was soon changed to Plott Creek, and the beautiful surrounding area later became known as Plott Valley. The towering mountains overlooking the valley would eventually come to be called the Plott Balsams. Henry Plott later extended his holdings to about 1,700 acres in the vicinity that now includes most of the Waynesville, Pigeon and Hazelwood, North Carolina area townships.

This is the area where the Plott hound would gain legendary status as one of the premier big game hunting dogs in the world.

Chapter Four

HOME IN THE MOUNTAINS

Henry Plott, his family and dogs flourished in their new mountain home in Plott Valley. Aside from the first winter that he spent there alone with his dogs, not much else is known of Henry's specific hunting exploits or his dogs. But family history has it that he quickly became a respected hunter, farmer and dog breeder in the area. And the Plott hounds quickly developed a fine reputation of their own as the best hunting dogs in the mountains. One of the original outbuildings from the old Plott homestead still stands in the valley today, and the homeplace itself remained in the Plott family until late into the twentieth century. Some Plott family members still live in the Plott Valley area, though, unfortunately, none to my knowledge are still raising hunting dogs.

By 1820, Henry and Lydia Plott had eleven children, eight boys (Osborne, Jonathan, Henry Jr., Enos, John T., Amos, George and David) and three girls (Caroline, Celinda and Peggy). Henry passed on his hunting and dog knowledge to the boys, most, if not all, of whom became fine hunters and dog men in their own right. Of these early nineteenth-century Plott men, Enos, David and Amos, in particular, would all gain fame in the Carolina mountains for their dogs and hunting skills.

Amos Plott's favorite Plott hound was a dog he named Porter. Porter helped Amos gain a reputation for annually bringing in the largest amount of bearskins and meat in the region. On a hunt in the Balsams in the mid-1800s, Porter and Amos encountered a particularly tough and extremely large bear that fatally wounded Porter. Amos was distraught over the loss of his prized dog. To honor him he named the site where he was killed after the hound. To this day, the gap near Maggie Valley, North Carolina, is known as Porter Die Gap.

Amos, like quite a few of the Plotts, myself included, was left-handed. This trait served him well, probably saving his life on another early bear hunt. The Plott legacy contends that Amos's dogs had struck a bear trail, and while being hotly pursued the wounded bruin sought refuge from them in a large hole where a tree had been uprooted.

Closely behind, Amos soon arrived to find his hounds holding the bear at bay in the hole. The bear was deeply entrenched there at an awkward angle and the dogs were unable to reach him. Amos surveyed the situation, and unable to get off a shot with

Von Plott and dogs at Plott Valley home. Note the old building behind him, supposedly dating back to the 1800 Henry Plott farm.

Porter Die Gap. Site near Maggie Valley, North Carolina. Named for Porter, the favorite Plott hound of Amos Plott, who was killed there by a bear in the mid-1800s.

his muzzleloading rifle, he decided his only option was to try and kill the bear with his knife. He then wrapped his right arm to provide it some protection, as he intended to use it as a shield while he attempted with his stronger left hand to kill the bruin with his knife. From the only angle available to him, a fierce fight ensued as Amos blocked with his right hand and attacked with his left. He was pretty badly ripped up, but he finally managed to kill the bear. Others in the party said that Amos was drenched in blood from head to toe and nearly bled to death as the hunting party returned to Plott Valley.

Amos fully recovered and continued to hunt and raise dogs until he was an old man. Family lore has it that he and his brother Enos also served as guides for Arnold Guyot, the noted Swiss geographer, on some of his research trips into the Smokies in 1856, 1857, 1859 and 1860, or at least those in the Balsam Mountain range.

Thomas Clingman and Dr. Elisha Mitchell were at that time feuding over what the highest mountains were in the Southeast, and Clingman enlisted Guyot to prove his point. Guyot, supposedly in appreciation for the help of the Plott men, named two mountains after them, Amos Plott Balsam and Enos Plott Balsam. Amos Plott Balsam, a towering 6,292-foot peak, is now known as Waterrock Knob. However, in an early Guyot map, dated 1864 in the Special Collections area of Hunter Library at Western Carolina University, it is indeed noted as Amos Plott Balsam. Amos Plott's cabin is still standing today in Maggie Valley, North Carolina, and his muzzleloading rifle remains a treasured family heirloom.

Original mid-1800s cabin of Amos Plott in Maggie Valley, North Carolina.

By the time of the Civil War, Henry and Lydia Plott's children, and in some cases grandchildren, had married and had large families of their own. They were spread mostly across Haywood County but were also in north Georgia and Clay County, North Carolina. As John Jackson notes in an article written in the American Plott Association's *2005 Brindle Book*, the Plott family seemed to have a knack for working with animals, and for establishing fine farms—one with a gristmill and a wheelwright shop. They not only were famous for their multipurpose Plott bear dogs, but also had the best riding horses, cattle, sheep and hogs. And they had also developed a reputation for having some of the best fighting chickens around. So these "bottomland mountaineers," as John Jackson cleverly calls them, were extremely talented folks.

By the start of the Civil War, the Plott dog had been in America for more than one hundred years, and it is here that I want to make another point regarding the breed. It is part of the Plott hound mystique that the family allowed very little, if any, outside breeding to occur during this time, and that even later, only a few outside infusions were allowed. I disagree with this, as do most dog experts that I have interviewed.

Robert Jones, age seventy-eight of Hahira, Georgia, and a founding member of the American Plott Association, as well as an honorary lifetime member, feels strongly about this. Mr. Jones told me at APA Breed Days in 2007 that he just did not see how this was possible. He is certainly qualified to make that assessment. In addition to being one of the first, if not *the* first, licensed hunting guides in the notorious Okeefenokee Swamp, he has bred and hunted Plott dogs since 1955, and with a degree in agriculture, he is very familiar with the science of animal husbandry.

He feels, as I do, that it would be virtually impossible to take five dogs from 1750 and keep that pack perfectly pure with no outside influences for more than one hundred years. This would be hard to do even in a strictly supervised modern clinical laboratory environment. But, I believe it would have been almost impossible to do on the wild American frontier, with dogs running loose in and around the wilderness for more than a century.

Now, that is not to say that the Plotts were not protective of their animals and were not very selective in how they were bred. I absolutely believe that they were. Like their German ancestors, the American Plotts were master dog breeders with unique animal husbandry skills. The family understood dominant and recessive genetics without even knowing those scientific terms. They simply bred for the results they wanted with proven producers, eliminating or culling any defective or weak stock that did not meet their standard. And I do believe that there had to be outside influences added to the bloodline from other breeds in America, just as I think was done earlier in Germany. But I don't believe that there were very many. I maintain that in an effort to ensure the purity of the breed, the Plott family was very selective and would allow only the best outside infusions into their line. To have kept the breed totally pure would have required them to allow nothing but inbreeding for more than one hundred years. This would have been difficult, to say the least, in the frontier environment in which the Plott family lived.

Inbreeding in the broadest sense of the term simply means mating within a family, usually sister to brother, offspring to parent, etc. Leon Whitney writes in *The Basis of Breeding* that this can also be known as "purification of stock," and that "anything further removed than first cousins cannot be considered inbreeding."

The Plott family had to subscribe to this theory, as well as linebreeding, to keep their lineage as pure as possible. But, I believe that due to culling stock that did not meet their standards, as well as simply losing dogs to illness and the many hazards of the frontier, the Plotts had to bring some outside stock into the line to preserve their lineage. We can only speculate as to what the specific makeup of this outside stock was. But just as with their German ancestors, the American Plott family would have sought out the best stock available that met their specific needs. They could then use their expert breeding skills to further refine the Plott hound lineage. There were certainly many options for them to choose from.

Robert Brookes arrived in America in 1650 with a pack of hunting dogs that were the forebears of several well-known strains of hounds, including the Walker, Trigg, July and Penn-Marydel foxhounds. By 1750, descendants of these dogs were spread across the American colonies and were readily available to the Plott family dog breeding pool, especially in the Piedmont of North Carolina.

Other English, French and Spanish settlers and soldiers also brought dogs to America before and after Brookes. But this is, again, an area where the Plott hound is unique in that its original bloodlines were of almost entirely Germanic origins, as opposed to the other dogs of the era, which we believe mostly came from English stock.

Cur dogs were widely available to the American Plott hound breeding pool, and after coming to America, they had evolved into several different types of curs, including the blackmouthed cur and the mountain cur. Surely the Plott family at some point incorporated quality cur bloodlines into the American Plott dog mix, just as their ancestors may have done earlier in Germany. And some notable Plott family members often referred to their Plott hounds as curs, so we must take that into consideration, too.

Two of the best documented early American examples of hunting dogs come first in 1752, from a diary entry, and later in 1760, from a newspaper report. The Moravian missonary Bishop Spangenburg noted in his diary written in 1752 that a settler along the Catawba River named Andreas Lambert "set his 8 or 9 bear dogs on some Indians" who had raided his farm. The *Pennsylvania Gazette* reports in an item dated May 1, 1760, that in mid-April a hunting party led by hunter, scout and local resident John Perkins had a fight with Indians near the Catawba River. The article states, "Mr. Perkin's dog followed one of the wounded Indians in the river, where he seized him, and held him fast till he [the Indian] was drowned."

The Plott family was almost certainly in the region by then, so these dogs possibly could have been Plott hounds or some of the other previously mentioned frontier breeds. In the case of Lambert's dogs, it is especially interesting to note that they were referred to specifically as "bear dogs." So maybe they were Plott hounds that were obtained from Johannes by his fellow German immigrant, Andreas Lambert. It is entirely possible that they could have been, but no one knows for sure.

In referring to the Plott hound in *The Encyclopedia of North Carolina*, William Powell states, "Like certain tools and weapons, dogs were developed [by European settlers and Indians] to meet specialized needs in different locales and times."

That is exactly my point.

So, just from these few examples, and there are many, many more, the Plott family had some fine breeding options to choose from when, or if, they chose to bring any outside influences into the Plott hound bloodline. More importantly, this stock was clearly available to them at the time, and in the various locations where they settled. Both Perkins and Lambert lived near where Johannes Plott eventually settled, close to the Catawba River in the foothills of Western North Carolina. And there were plenty of other dog breeding choices for the Plott family to choose from scattered throughout other parts of North Carolina as well.

To add further mystery to this possible American mix, Taylor Crockett stated in a 1985 *Wildlife in North Carolina* article that the Plott hound had some wolf blood in its lineage. Crockett recalled: "Old man Von [this was a misprint and actually was John] Plott told me that there was a big apple tree down there on the farm where they settled [Plott Valley]. And they'd tie their dog to that big apple tree, tie out a bitch you know, and let the male wolf come in and they'd get their half wolf that way."

He added, "They [the old-time Plott family] said when you got your half-wolf out of a sensible, good natured dog, the dogs were not so wild, were more dog like and could be handled. If it was the other way around it didn't work."

Crockett went on to say that early on he had some Plott dogs himself with some wolf in their bloodlines. They had slanted yellow eyes, but there were few, if any, left by the mid-1900s. Crockett was well known as an honest man and he was friends with Von Plott and other famous breeders and hunters of his era, so I have to believe this to be true. Plus, as we will see in Chapter Five, Von's father, Montraville Plott, was known to have once had a pet wolf at his Plott Valley homeplace.

This again leads me to conclude that the Plott family combined their expertise in dog breeding skills with a very few, but select, outside blood lines (maybe even a wolf or two) to further expand, preserve and refine the early dogs first produced by their German forefathers. In combining the best traits of the European breeds with those available to them on the American frontier, the family produced the ultimate prototype for the most illustrious big game dog the world had ever seen—the early American version of the old-time Plott bear hound. And it would be Montraville Plott who would be instrumental in making this happen.

Chapter Five

MONTRAVILLE

John Plott, the seventh son of Henry and Lydia, was born in 1813. Along with his seven brothers, it is assumed that he had managed to maintain and grow the Plott dog pack through the turbulent Civil War years and well into the second half of the nineteenth century. Like his father Henry, we don't know a lot of specific details about John Plott, but Plott family members maintain that like his more famous brothers, he was a master dog breeder and hunter. Tradition has it that his father, Henry, thought enough of John to leave his pack and breeding stock to him when he died. We do have a photo of John and it shows a lean mountaineeer, with a kind, clean-shaven face and a slight, but warm, smile. We know, too, that he was married to Louisa Reeves and that they had four children. The most famous of these was a son, Montraville, who was born on February 19, 1850.

By the time of Montraville Plott's birth, the Plott hound was well known throughout the mountain and foothill areas of Western North Carolina, but it was little known outside of the region. Montraville, or "Mont" as he was more commonly known, would play an important role in the breed gaining national recognition.

Mont married Julia McClure on Christmas Day in 1875. Their union produced ten children, five of them boys. The youngest and oldest sons would become nationally known for their hunting and dog breeding abilities. The oldest, John A., and his son "Little" George and the youngest brother, Vaughn or "Von," were the most famous. But their other brothers, especially George Fred, known as "Big" George, as well as Samuel Cole, would all become well-known Plott dog men in their own right The remaining brother, Robert Ellis, was apparently never actively involved in the dog trade.

Mont, like other Plotts, was not only a fine farmer and hunter, but also, in a family of exceptional animal breeders, was known as one of the best. He passed these skills and secrets down to his boys, especially John and Von. Though the family had long been protective in keeping the Plott dog lineage as pure as possible, Mont was nevertheless well known for his generosity in sharing litters of his pups with neighbors and friends.

There has been much debate among breed experts as to whether there actually ever were any strictly kept breeding "secrets" among the Plott family, and if so, whether

John T. Plott, brother of Amos, Enos and David Plott; father of Montraville Plott; and grandfather of "Big Five" icons John A. and H.V. "Von" Plott.

Plott family patriarch Montraville "Mont" Plott as a young man, taken around 1870.

they were extremely protective of them. No one can prove it either way. The Plotts surely weren't adverse to sharing pups with friends, nor later were they reluctant to sell them across the country. But I maintain that while perhaps the Plott family had no breeding secrets per se, they definitely had superb breeding skills. I believe too that they were extremely proud, and at least to some extent protective, of their animals and their lineage.

Von Plott recalled in a 1973 *Sport Afield* article that "people would ride in here [Plott Valley] on a mule with a tow sack and they'd go home with pups. They'd come for miles around to get one of those brindle dogs. People had to have them to keep their families safe from wild animals."

In 1976 Von told the *Foxfire* staff: "People used to come over here when I was a little ole youngun, I helped him [Mont] fool with the dogs. I've seen them come by mule and horseback and get pups in a sack, and leave to go back to Georgia, and Murphy and that section. He just gave them to them. He'd raise a bunch, and have more than he wanted, so he'd give them to a few fellers."

While Mont was generous in sharing his stock, he recognized from an early age the value of perpetuating the Plott dog line, maybe even more so than anyone in the family before that time. According to Plott family tradition, Mont apparently was fiercely devoted to keeping the line as pure as possible, with only the best infusion of outside bloodlines permitted, and then only rarely and under his supervison. He spent his entire life dedicated to this goal of staying true to the Plott lineage. And his sons, especially John and Von, and his grandson, "Little" George, shared this dream.

It was in 1884 that the generosity of Mont Plott would result in one of the few documented outside infusions to the Plott hound lineage. There are many versions of this story, and as I said before, I believe there were other carefully supervised outside infusions as well. But none was more controversial, or as well documented, as that of the leopard dog. Following is the version that most breed authorities I interviewed agree is true.

Elijah Crow, a hunter and dog breeder, reportedly from Rabun Gap in the mountains of north Georgia, was well aware of the fame of the Plott hound and perhaps even hunted with Mont Plott. Mont clearly must have liked and trusted him, because in 1884, according to his son John, Mont allowed Crow to borrow a Plott stud dog to breed with his leopard hounds. These lep dogs had developed an excellent reputation as bear dogs. They were known to have a bluish gray, spotted coat, with somewhat longer and thicker hair than a Plott hound. It was from this spotted coat that their "leopard" nickname was derived.

We should first clarify just what the leopard hound was, as this is one of the foremost reasons for the confusion surrounding this story. Many people have said that this dog was simply a leopard cur or even a Catahoula leopard dog. Most dog experts agree that it was neither. Considering the known physical characteristics of this outcross, the leopard dog was almost certainly some type of foxhound, maybe a July, Walker, Trigg or Penn-Marydel foxhound. It was possibly even some mix of the four, or perhaps a foxhound-cur mix. This is somewhat ironic in that Mont usually disliked hounds, yet the skills and traits of the lep dogs evidently were impressive enough for him to overlook this.

Plott's Lep, a John Plott favorite and a classic example of the leopard-colored Plott hound.

As we discussed in Chapter Four, these breeds had been in America for a long time and were readily available and commonly used in the area. But while this issue will continue to be debated for years, the end result of this cross was that about a year later Crow returned to Plott Valley with the stud dog he had borrowed and one of the pups he had sired. This male pup was named Old Thunderer because he had a "million-dollar mouth." Old Thunderer was a notable addition to the Plott pack but unfortunately later died from a rattlesnake bite.

However, before Old Thunderer died, Mont bred this one-half lep and one-half Plott to a pure Plott brindle female and they whelped seven puppies. Four of these pups were leopard in appearance and three were brindle females. Perhaps due to his aversion to

The Mark Reece family with Montraville Plott–bred Plott hound Fleet on far right. This photo, taken in 1906, is thought to be the earliest known photo of a Plott hound in existence. Fleet was born in either 1896 or 1898.

"houndy" dogs, Mont still was not pleased with the dogs and gave five of them to the Reece brothers, Brice and Mark, who lived near Sunburst on the Pigeon River, south of Plott Valley. The Reece brothers were well known as two of the best bear hunters in Haywood County, a county famous for them.

Even though Mont apparently did not care for them, John Plott later said that the two lep pups his family kept subsequently became great bear dogs and were notably fierce fighters. However, one of these dogs was killed, and Mont eventually gave the remaining hound to the Reece brothers, too. The Reece boys evidently had great success with their lep Plotts and continued to hunt and breed them for years.

One of the earliest pictures of a Plott dog on record was taken with the Reece family and their dogs in 1906. It is a rare and extremely unusual photo because the dog on the far right is probably the best, and perhaps the only, picture in existence of a nineteenth-century Montraville Plott–bred old-time Plott hound. The dog's name was Fleet and at the time of the photo it was said to be between eight and ten years old. This would put his birth date between 1896 and 1898. However, to avoid confusion, I would add that Fleet was not a lep-colored Plott but was instead a prime example of an original old-time Plott hound.

Perhaps it was because of his disappointment with this outcross, or maybe for other unknown reasons, but Mont was especially adamant that the Plott dogs were never to be considered as hounds. As Taylor Crockett noted in Chapter Two, Mont would get extremely angry if anyone ever did this. When Mont was an old man, Wesley Ingles, who lived in the Reems Creek area of Buncombe County, North Carolina, innocently made the mistake of asking Mont "if it was true that the Plott hounds were the best bear hounds ever?" Mont supposedly leapt from his chair and angrily replied, "They're not HOUNDS! They are CURS!"

Apparently he did not want his dogs to be associated with the "houndy" traits that characterized most hound breeds. He evidently preferred, instead, the more cur-like traits of the multipurpose early dog discussed previously in Chapter Two. Mont made sure that none of his pack had any of these hound traits, and he would cull them if they did. He was completely devoted to these brindle-cur type dogs, for he felt that the end results clearly spoke for themselves. There are few, if any, that can argue with his assessment. But we unfortunately know very little of the reasoning behind his apparent specific dislike for dogs with "houndy" traits. This is especially perplexing due to his youngest son Von's affection for dogs of this type.

APA charter member John Jackson wrote in *Full Cry* magazine, as well as in the 2006 *APA Yearbook*, that "as far as Plott dog history is concerned, he [Mont] is probably the most legendary and colorful character of the entire Plott family." Jackson added, "While other Plotts have left indelible marks in the records of Plott dog history, no one has exceeded Mont in this regard…For all intents and purposes Mont Plott IS brindle bear dog history."

Considering his family roots, it is easy to see where, and from whom, Mont learned his hunting and animal husbandry skills. These skills alone would guarantee his rightful place in Plott hound and Plott family history. But, as Jackson describes so well, "Mont's main claim to fame rested in the type dog he used to hunt. This was the Plott cur, a gritty, close fighting, quickly moving, agile, aggressive, iron willed, chop mouthed, warm nosed dog that gave no quarter and expected none."

Jackson continues:

> *The most impressive quality of these outstanding dogs however, was not their ability to readily and fearlessly mix it up with large and dangerous animals, but rather their intelligence. The dogs seemed to have an innate ability to bond with their owners and seemed to possess the unusual capability of knowing what the hunter was thinking or needed. There just seemed to be a unique bond between these dogs and their masters that few other breeds had.*

This intelligence carried over not only to the field or hunting trail, but also to the farm as well. Leo, one of Taylor Crockett's favorite Plott hounds, had exceptional herding skills. According to Taylor, Leo was as fine and fierce a bear or boar dog as there ever was and came from primarily Evans and Cable family bloodlines. But Leo could also round up Crockett's baby shoats and gently bring them to their pen, counting them as he did so.

Mont's dogs were so well trained and intelligent that he would hunt bear while armed only with a single-shot black powder pistol. He would allow the dogs to corner or bay the bear, holding its attention, as he charged into the fracas killing the animal with his primitive, fifty-caliber cap-and-ball handgun. John Plott said that his father killed 211 bears in his lifetime using this method, and the pistol still remains in the Plott family today.

Mont once kept a pet wolf at his homeplace, and, according to his son John, he sometimes bred a female Plott dog to wolves. It was probably not this pet wolf—though I suppose it could have been—but there is another story regarding a wolf that is worthy of sharing. It seems that Mont was once scouting for bear sign high above the Plott homeplace on Eagles Nest Mountain. He had arranged for his wife, Julia, to release a few of his prized dogs when he signaled her from the peak. Julia received the signal and released the pack as planned. Off they went, tearing up the mountain, hot on the trail of their master and the bear sign that they knew would be waiting for them when they found him. The pet wolf was tied and became quite agitated, wanting to join the Plott dogs on the hunt. He struggled for a while to free himself from his chain, but by the time he did, the Plott dogs were long gone. Still, the wolf attemped in vain to catch up, but he quickly grew frustrated and returned back home. When he got there, angry I guess from missing out on the chase, he tore into Mrs. Plott's freshly washed laundry, which was hanging outside to dry, ripping it to shreds.

This proved to be a fatal mistake for the poor wolf, as Mrs. Plott was not going to put up with anyone or anything messing up her hard work. She screamed at the wolf to no avail. Angrily, she grabbed the first thing handy, in this case a frying pan (though some say a fireplace shovel) and went after the wolf. Without thinking once about her own safety, for this was after all still a dangerous wild animal, she proceeded to beat the wolf with the frying pan. Still unfazed, the animal continued to tear into her freshly washed

Muzzleloading, single-shot, black powder pistol used by Montraville Plott to kill 211 bears while hunting with his Plott hounds.

Mrs. Montraville Plott, the former Julia McClure, who once killed a wolf with a frying pan.

clothes, snapping at Mrs. Plott. She was not about to tolerate that and proceeded to kill the wolf with her frying pan.

Von Plott, in 1976, recalled to the *Foxfire* staff a story regarding his family and yet another "domesticated" wild animal. In the late 1800s and early 1900s the first influx of tourists hit the mountains near Plott Valley. They either stayed in nearby Waynesville or at one of the lodges on Eagles Nest Mountain. Looking for entertainment, some of these tourists paid a local man, Jim Thomas, to bring his pet bear to the lodge. Thomas would release the bear and turn some dogs on it so that the tourists could see a simulated "real bear hunt." Word soon got out amongst the locals, and quite a crowd gathered to see this event—so many, in fact, that lots of folks had climbed trees to get a better view. One big sycamore tree in particular was literally filled with spectators hanging from the limbs. Mont, along with his wife, one of their babies and three Plott hounds on leads, were also in attendance. According to Von, his dad had no intention of participating in this farce, but like the other locals came only for entertainment.

Much to the delight of the tourists the bear was freed and dogs, though not Mont's, were also released, and the chase began. The bear circled the crowd and disappeared into the woods. Shortly thereafter, to the crowd's dismay, the bruin charged back toward them from the opposite side of the timber with no dogs in sight. With the other dogs lost or afraid to pursue the angry, rampaging bear, Julia Plott, fearing for her baby, told Mont to turn the Plott dogs loose. Someone else in the crowd also beseeched him to do so, yelling, "By God, turn the Plotts on him!"

Mont did just that. According to Von, the Plott dogs, led by a gyp named Bute, quickly turned the bear as it headed straight up the big sycamore tree full of spectators. Von said there were at least twenty-five men up that big tree and that they began to run the limbs and jump off them like frightened squirrels. Once clear of spectators, the Plott dogs kept the bear treed until the other dogs suddenly regained their courage and joined them. Mont then took his Plott dogs and his family home. The bear's owner and the other dogs were left to resolve the situation after the Plott hounds had yet again vividly demonstrated their superior skills and courage. Bute was probably the great-great-grandmother, or even great-great-great-grandmother, of another well-known Plott hound, also known as Bute, who was on the famous 1935 Branch Rickey Hazel Creek bear hunt. We will discuss this hunt in Chapter Eight.

About 1885, Montraville Plott's friendship with another local pioneer family, the Phillips, would result in some of the purest Plott dog stock ever bred. These dogs were the forefathers of todays Crockett-Plotts, still one of the best remaining examples of early Plott dog stock. Thomas Clingman Phillips and his family lived in the Caney Fork area of nearby Jackson County, North Carolina. They visited Plott Valley regularly. On one of these visits Phillips obtained some pure Plott pups from Mont Plott. Phillips swore that these were the best dogs he had ever seen and vowed that he would never have another type of dog or breed his dogs to anything but a Mont Plott–bred dog. Phillips developed a fine pack of his own hounds, and he would yearly ride by horseback to Mont's place to continue the breeding cycle, further ensuring the purity of his stock.

Phillips later moved his family to the remote and wild Tusquitee area of Clay County, North Carolina. He recalled that it took three days by wagon to make this difficult trip,

Taylor Crockett's Boss. Killed by a boar at age eleven. He was a fine example of Evans/Plott stock.

and that they could not have made it safely there without his Plott dogs. Phillips had a huge bull named Noble on his new farm, which normally was docile, but one day unexpectedly and savagely attacked his young daughter. Before Phillips could grab a weapon or reach his daughter to save her, two of his Plott dogs charged the raging animal and latched on to its ears dragging it to the ground, saving his daughter's life.

The Evans and Cheek families also lived in Clay County and were related to the Phillips. Over the years, Mr. Phillips gave some of his pups to both families, with the understanding that they in return would keep the breed as pure as he did. By all accounts they kept their promise.

Phillips continued his yearly pilgrimage to Plott Valley long after moving to Clay County, making the hard ride there from the late 1880s until about 1924, when he was

Crockett's Leo. A Taylor Crockett favorite and a fine multipurpose farm and hunting dog. Note the heavy coat and tail and strong Phillips/Evans/Cable old-time influences.

too old to endure the trip. Even then he remained true to his word and would breed only within his own pack, using linebreeding and inbreeding techniques he most likely learned from Mont.

Even as an older man, Mont Plott remained active by hunting and working with his dogs, sometimes suprising even his own sons with his exceptional knowledge and insight. "Big" George and Von Plott told author Michael Frome, in his book *Strangers in High Places*, of a time when a New Yorker had come south to North Carolina to hunt and buy dogs from Mont. According to the Plott brothers, most of their older, experienced dogs were "about fought out," and six had been killed by the notorious rogue bear known as Old Reelfoot. The brothers were concerned that the only remaining dogs they had to hunt with were younger and inexperienced, having never fought a bear before.

Big George recalled that his father instructed him to take the young dogs anyway and assured him that they would be fine. Big George felt otherwise, thinking instead that the young dogs would surely be embarrassed and humiliated on the hunt. Nevertheless, he followed Mont's instructions and took their visitor on a bear hunt into the Snowbird Mountains near Robbinsville, North Carolina.

Montraville Plott at about age seventy in 1920 with Plott hound pup.

Upon arriving and striking a bear trail, Big George said:

There were a big fight. The bear got in a hole. The dogs charged in one after another. They got beat up pretty bad, but they stayed at it, and charged until they got him. I never had any question about my daddy after that. If a dog would not stay all day, my daddy killed them. He had to stay and fight, he had to stay with the bear at the tree. This breed of dog won't quit, he may get clawed and chewed, but he'll be back next week. It is one with plenty of gut. The man who isn't game isn't fit to have him.

By the time of his death in 1924, Montraville Plott was respected and well known throughout the southern highlands for many notable achievements. He had raised a fine family and had a beautiful farm of almost two thousand acres, filled with prized livestock and dogs. He was a legendary bear hunter credited with 211 kills. Most importantly, he was known by his neighbors to have had an impeccable reputation as an honest and generous man.

But as impressive as all these achievements were, they pale in comparison to his greatest accomplishment, which was perpetuating the legacy of his family and their amazing Plott dogs. Like his forefathers before him, he had not only lived a life devoted to maintaining and carefully improving the lineage of the family pack, but also he had instilled that same fierce devotion in his sons, who would carry it deep into the twentieth century.

Equally as impressive were the relationships Mont and his family developed with individuals and families scattered throughout the mountains, whose names read like an Appalachian history hall of fame: the Cable, Blevins, Reece, Evans, Phillips, Hannah, Denton, Gregory, Arrwood, Cruse, Wiggins, Martin, Russell, Ellerd, Monteith and Orr families, among others, all famous mountain clans. These families played instrumental parts in perpetuating the Plott breed. Later on they would directly and indirectly be tied not only to the Plott family, but also to other legendary Plott dog figures, like Taylor Crockett, Isaiah Kidd and Gola Ferguson, in helping to further advance the Plott dog breed.

It was by sharing his fine dogs with these famous families and individuals, combined with his own steadfast dedication to the breed, that Montraville Plott became one of the most, if not *the* most, important figure in Plott hound history. And he certainly was one of the most colorful. We will discuss some of these other families and individuals, as well as their contributions to the Plott dog legacy, in the next few chapters. But first, let's take a closer look at the old-time Plott bear hound.

Chapter Six

THE OLD-TIME PLOTT BEAR HOUND

Unfortunately, we have only one possible picture of these nineteenth-century dogs and can only base our impressions of them on what little written and oral history has survived, as well as from the opinions of historians such as John Jackson. Jackson has studied the subject extensively and was a protégé of the late aforementioned Taylor Crockett, who actually knew some of the early Plott family. Crockett developed his own strain of Plott dogs from stock he received from the Plott, Evans and Cable families, as well as from other notable early pioneer families.

We are fortunate, from about 1900 on, to have some good records and photos of Plott hounds that we can be reasonably sure are indicative examples of the early breed. We also have records and photos of the breeders that were devoted to keeping the stock true to the early bloodlines. Some of the best photos of these early dogs come from the Plott family themselves on various hunts and at their homes in Plott Valley. Photos of John Plott and his son Little George are especially good points of reference. And even though John's younger brother Von later preferred and developed a more "houndy" type of Plott, some early photos of his dogs are fine examples, too. A 1938 photo of Von's dogs Dan and Scott shows superb old-time Plott specimens. Those two dogs alone were in on fifty-six bear kills in one year. More excellent photos of early dogs come from the Cable and Blevins families, as well as from Taylor Crockett and Gola Ferguson, all of whom we will discuss in more detail in later chapters.

It is also important to note that when we use the term "early dogs," we are referring to a time period running from the mid- to late eighteenth century until the early to mid-twentieth century. We use such a broad span of time here due to the fact that the area and lifestyle of the Western North Carolina mountains did not change tremendously during that time. Well into the twentieth century, most folks still farmed, hunted and were incredibly self-sufficient, living in a lot of ways like mountain people had for nearly two hundred years. They depended on these early types of multipurpose Plott hounds to help them survive.

Taylor Crockett provides an excellent example of this. He was born in 1908, and remembered that well into the early 1900s, farmers still let their hogs and cattle run

Plott's Scott on left and Dan on right. Both are fine examples of old-time Plott hounds and superb hunting dogs. They were on the 1935 Branch Rickey hunt and were in on fifty-six bear kills during one year of their illustrious hunting careers.

Individual photo of Plott's Dan, one of the most proficient Plott stud dogs of all time. Sire to such famous Plotts as Dale Brandenburger's Joe and Ruby, as well as Everette Weems's Suzi.

wild. Fences were built around fields to keep cattle and hogs out, not in, just as it had been done more than one hundred years earlier. The farmers would mark or notch the ears of their stock to identify them, and they would have yearly roundups to bring the animals in for slaughter or market. Crockett recalled that these folks would use their Plott hounds to herd the cattle and hogs and bring them back to the farm. They would use these same dogs to hunt bear and other big game, as well as to protect their family and farm from human and animal predators.

The late Jake Waldroop's relatives, the Cruse family, were from the Nantahala area of the Great Smokies, between Aquone and Andrews, North Carolina. Jake recalled in *Foxfire Five* that his uncle Wint Cruse had gotten his first Plott hounds in the late 1800s directly from the Plott family—most likely Montraville Plott. He said these six pups grew into remarkable bear hunting dogs, but noted that they had other skills too:

> *They was good for coons. They would take them out and if there wasn't no bear for them to get after, why, they'd curl up a coon. They was just jacks of all trades, them Plott hounds was. They'd run wildcats some. And wolves, wolves in the mountains—they said they could find where a wolf was. We'd go up there in the morning, and it wasn't no time 'til we'd have him killed. They'd [Plott dogs] fight him 'til he couldn't travel. He'd just have to give up and then we'd go up there and shoot him [wolf] to stop it.*

Multipurpose dogs indeed.

John Jackson describes these early dogs as "iron willed and feisty." Crockett called them "aggressive, fast on the track and gritty," with a ton of what he considered as "go power-enthusiasm, and lots of heart and desire." Steve Fielder, American Kennel Club vice-president, avid hunter and Plott hound man, notes the "undying courage of the breed" and the dogs' "extraordinary intelligence and desire." Plott man Randy Wolfe states simply that these early dogs "had a head full of sense."

They also possessed an uncommon bond with, and loyalty to, their owners, being as Taylor Crockett called them in *Foxfire Five*, "one man dogs." By this he meant that they would respond only to their owners, no one else. Some hunters saw this as a weakness and would not use them because of it. Plott enthusiasts treasured this trait.

Crockett recalled in *Foxfire Five* that one of his dogs was so protective of him that it would not allow a friend of his to get into his car if he was not there. One of the Crockett family Plott dogs often served as a baby sitter to Taylor's younger brother, John Stuart Ramsey Crockett, who was eighteen years his junior. Crockett said, "When he was just a toddler, I had an old Plott female. We lived on this farm and had big old turkey gobblers running around, geese, and a big old sow or bull might get out. You had to watch kids, you know? He'd [his brother] get out of sight, but I didn't have to worry because that old female stayed right with him, and if a chicken or anything else got near him, she'd put it in high gear!"

Sam George of White Sulphur Springs, West Virginia—a respected Plott man, hunter and honorary lifetime APA member, who has hunted and raised Plott dogs for over fifty years—remembers much the same thing with his Plott dogs looking after his daughter Lisa when she was a young child.

"Uncle" Mark Cathey, celebrated Smoky Mountain outdoorsman, bear hunter and Plott hound advocate. Dog pictured is probably not a Plott hound.

Stories abound of hunters being injured or even unexpectedly dying in the woods and their Plott dogs staying with their master until another family member was called to quiet them. Probably the best one of these stories involves legendary Swain County, North Carolina outdoorsman Mark Cathey. "Uncle Mark," as he was sometimes fondly called, was a much celebrated Great Smokies trout fisherman and bear hunter. He was born in 1871 and was a lifelong bachelor who devoted his life to outdoor pursuits. During his lifetime he earned a living as a logger, herder, trapper and as a hunting and fishing guide. Cathey was a dedicated Plott hound man. He would hunt bear with no other type of dog and kept Plott dogs his entire life.

Cathey's hunting buddy, Sam Hunnicut, a fine outdoorsman himself, confirmed this in his memoir *Twenty Years of Hunting and Fishing in the Great Smoky Mountains*, published in 1951. He noted that Cathey would use only Plott dogs, and Hunnicut named three of them by name: Dread, Jolly and Old Wheeler. Mark killed his first bear at age twelve with a muzzleloading rifle, and by his own count, he killed fifty-seven bears with Plott hounds that he owned over his lifetime. This may have been a conservative figure, as Cathey was known to have been a very humble and modest man.

In October 1944, at the age of seventy-three, Cathey took one of his dogs with him back in the mountains for a squirrel hunt. After not returning by dark, his sister became worried and a search party was sent to find him. Sometime after midnight, he was found sitting under a large oak tree, his rifle across his lap, dead from an apparent heart attack. His loyal Plott hound was still at his side, trying to protect him and keep him warm.

Mark Cathey, along with his friend Horace Kephart, is buried on a hill overlooking Bryson City, North Carolina. His tombstone has the finest epitaph I have ever seen for any sportsman. It reads: "Beloved Hunter and Fisherman was himself caught by the Gospel Hook just before the season closed for good."

Another story worth sharing regarding the loyalty of the early Plott hounds involves yet another bigger than life mountain man, Aquilla "Quill" Rose. The world's most gifted novelists or Hollywood scriptwriters could never have created a character as colorful as the real-life Quill Rose. Quill was a tall, wiry, broad-shouldered, handsome man, with long dark hair and a beard. He was well known for his hunting skills, moonshine making, fiddle playing and good sense of humor. Rose was once described as being "good-natured, but of desperate character when aroused." Quill was married to a Cherokee woman named Vicie, and with their children, they lived far up Eagle Creek in the Great Smoky Mountains on the Tennessee–North Carolina border.

Horace Kephart mentions Quill prominently in his book *Our Southern Highlanders* and hunted with him a few times, though Quill was an old, but still active, man by then. Kephart termed the area where Quill and his family lived as "the back of beyond," and rightfully so, as today this area in the Great Smokies National Park remains some of the wildest country remaining in eastern America.

Quill was also one of the handful of white members of Colonel Will Thomas's famous Cherokee Legion, serving for the Confederacy during the Civil War. After the war, in addition to farming, blacksmithing, moonshining and running his own gristmill, Rose further supplemented his income by using his Plott dogs to hunt bears and wolves, selling the wolf hides to the government for the five-dollar bounty they offered, up until 1891.

Quill, like Mark Cathey, was a devoted Plott hound man and would use no other dogs to hunt with. I suspect he got his dogs from the Cable family who lived nearby on Hazel Creek. Quill told Wilbur Zeigler and Ben Grosscup, authors of *In the Heart of the Alleghenies*, in about 1883, that two of his favorite Plott hounds were named Ring and Snap, and that in 1882, he had killed between eight and ten bears with these dogs. In seasons prior to that he had averaged about twenty bear kills a season.

Quill not only enjoyed making liquor, but evidently was never one to shy away from sampling it, either. The story goes that Rose left his home one day accompanied by two of his Plott dogs, possibly Ring and Snap, bound for Proctor, North Carolina, where he planned to catch the train to visit friends for the day in Bryson City, North Carolina. When he arrived to board the train, he suddenly realized he could not take his hounds with him, but having no one to leave them with, he was faced with the dilemma of what to do with the animals. As the train began to leave, Quill removed his hat, threw it to the ground and ordered his Plott dogs to guard it until he returned. Rose quickly boarded the train and left for Bryson City thinking the hounds would be fine until his return later that same day.

Quill soon arrived in Bryson City, where he met his friends and had a bit too much to drink. Two days later he arrived back home after catching a ride with one of his buddies. When he got home, he asked his wife Vicie where his dogs were? She replied that she did not know. But she reminded him that he had left with them two days earlier. Quill then remembered his mistake and rushed back to Proctor. When he got there, he found his Plott hounds guarding his hat right where he had left them two days before!

Now, Quill, like a lot of hunters, was known at times to embellish the truth a bit when it came to his dogs and adventures. So while his hounds may or may not have actually been there for two whole days, it is still nonetheless impressive that they would stay there as he had ordered for any extended period of time.

So what did these loyal, tenacious, feisty and intelligent dogs look like, and how did they perform on the game trail?

Outdoor writer Jim Gasque visited the "Von" Plott farm in January 1947, and he described the Plott hounds there in his book *Hunting and Fishing in the Great Smokies*. Gasque called them "large boned dogs, with broad chests and medium length ears." And he added that the canines weighed between forty-five and sixty-five pounds, although one tipped the scales at sixty-seven pounds. Gasque then took specific height measurements, noting that the adult dogs ranged from twenty-four to twenty-seven inches in height, measured from ground to shoulder, and a four-month-old pup measured seventeen inches high. Gasque further stated: "The color of the pure strain of these [Plott] hounds is a dark molish or bluish, with more or less brindle mixed in. Some of them are of almost a solid dark color, while others may have a prominent brindle chest and a greater or lesser belt of brindle across the back. While this is the predominant color, about ten percent of the puppies have a buckskin color when born, which they keep through life."

Though, in some respects, Von later had a more distinctly "houndy" strain of Plotts, these 1947 dogs were more representative of the old-time Plott hounds. Furthermore, they are proof that buckskin is indeed a legitimate breed standard color. Unfortunately only the American Kennel Club and Professional Kennel Club currently officially recognize it as such.

Jake Waldroop remembered the old-time Plott hound as follows: "Plotts was big dogs. I imagine them dogs would weigh anywhere from sixty to seventy-five to eighty pounds. They was big, large, heavy dogs. Most of them had big, coarse mouths. You could just hear them from one of these mountains to the other one, barking and treeing."

John Jackson best describes these early Plott hounds as "shorter eared, with ears higher on their head than your usual hound, and the ears having erectile capabilities causing them to raise slightly when excited." With harder winters back then, their hair was thicker and and a bit longer than dogs of today. They still remained a short-haired dog, with medium legs and a slightly flagged tail. Their coat color ranged from various brindle shades, including brown, black, red, yellow and gray, to buckskin, but the brindle colors were prominent. Another early trait was the "frosty" mouth, an appearance that gave some dogs a white muzzle. These dogs had none of the loose-skinned, long, floppy-eared traits of your traditional hound. They were very muscular, but extremely lean and athletic looking. Steve Fielder says that you could almost hang a ring on the hipbone of some of these early dogs and that old-timers sometimes used this as a means to evaluate the body of a top dog.

Jackson adds that they had fairly broad chests with a bigger and a bit more blocky head than your usual hound. The hounds had prominent dark brown or hazel eyes, and no drooping eye lids. They were "hot-nosed, hot tracking" dogs. These dogs had a "chop mouth," a more staccato type of bark or bay, versus the long, drawn out howls of a "bawl mouth" hound. Being more hot-nosed, they were quick to tree and did not prefer long, drawn out hunts, but were known as being quick, evasive and efficient fighters. Yet, even still, many had the capability and tenacity to stay on a game trail for extended periods of time.

Von Plott recalled a dog of his named Little John that treed a bear on Saturday morning and was still at the same tree barking at noon on Monday. Still, this was the exception, rather than the rule, as the early Plott hound normally prefered to jump a hot trail fast and end the hunt fairly quickly. Most latter-day Plott dogs are more "cold-nosed" with better cold trail tracking skills.

Even as protective of their owners and gentle with children as these early dogs were, they were still extremely aggressive fighters. The Plott hound could be "vicious" as Jake Waldrop described them in *Foxfire Five* and willing to fight a bear, hog, wolf, bobcat or panther to the death if turned upon.

Von Plott, who obtained his first Plott pup at age ten, and owned by his own account over a thousand dogs in his lifetime, agreed with this assessment. Von said in 1973 that the breed is by nature easygoing and gentle until provoked, when they will then fight another animal to the death. Plott added that as a result, the breed sometimes developed an unfair reputation among other dog owners for starting fights with their dogs. He said that he had seen few Plott hounds start fights with other dogs, but that they would almost always finish them.

Plott dogs could also sometimes be dangerous to each other, as Taylor Crockett noted in a 1983 *Wildlife in North Carolina* article. He stated, "Some people's objection to the

Plott is that they are a little bit hard to handle, and they are if you don't know how to handle them. You have to keep them apart or they will fight amongst themselves. I've lost more dogs, had them kill each other, than I have lost to game."

John Jackson says that Plott hounds then, and now, unlike most other dogs, are unique in that "they will hold a grudge." By that he means that most other pups or dogs when bullied by a bigger, stronger canine will back down, and even after they are grown, will remain intimidated by the bully dog from their past. Not the Plott hound. Even after taking a beating or backing down from the bully, the Plott pup will bide its time, holding a grudge, not forgetting the beating it took, and when it is older and stronger, it will then take its revenge. Full-grown Plott dogs also possess this trait and will almost always seek vengeance on another dog that has hurt or wronged them.

It is important to note that when describing a Plott hound, most folks believe that the primary defining characteristic of the breed is their distinctive brindle coat. This is really only a small part of what makes up a true old-time Plott dog. Granted, most of these early dogs did indeed have beautiful brindle coats of various shades, and Plott enthusiasts still take pride in this. But simply having a brindle coat is not what made these dogs special. Many dog breeds share this quality. It is, instead, the unique character traits of the early Plott hound that set it apart from all others. Their grit, their tenacity, their multipurpose skills and most of all, their intelligence, is what made them then, and now, such a valued commodity to their owners.

With all of these unique attributes, it is easy to see why the Plott hound was so popular among these early pioneers, and why the dog so quickly spread among a network of elite mountain clans that lived throughout the southern mountain empire. It was these celebrated Appalachian families, all with direct or indirect ties to Montraville Plott and his family, who would play integral roles in the further improvement and refinement of the already legendary Plott bear hound. Let's take a look at some of these unique families.

Chapter Seven

THE MOUNTAIN EMPIRE

By the end of his life, Montraville Plott's fine dogs were spread across a still sparsely populated mountain empire, within a network of several well-known early pioneer families. All of these families would use the dogs for hunting, as well as for protecting their families, just as the Plott family had done for almost 175 years. Though change was indeed slow in coming to the mountain empire, there were two specific events that would profoundly impact the hunting culture of the region. First was the arrival of a brand-new big game animal to the southern mountains, the wild boar. Second was the network of families who had gotten dogs from the Plott family and then went on to develop their own strain of Plott hounds.

Plenty of wild animals still roamed the woods, although the bear population had been thinned down some due to the expertise of local hunters and their Plott dogs. But in 1912, a new big game animal was introduced to the empire, really by accident. Feral hogs—pigs that either permanently escaped from farms or from the annual livestock roundups—had roamed the mountains since the arrival of the first white settlers to the area. Once they went wild, they could be dangerous in their own right and were often hunted. Yet they were meek in comparison to the wild boars that came to Graham County, North Carolina, in 1912, and spread rapidly across the region.

Word was gradually beginning to reach the outside world regarding the beauty of the mountain empire, as well as the great hunting available in the region. Logging company officials often brought friends or clients into the area to hunt. It was one of these companies, Whiting Manufacturing, that acquired 1,600 acres in 1912 to build a European-style hunting preserve in the Snowbird Mountains about twenty miles from Robbinsville, North Carolina. Part of their plan was to fence this huge tract in, and stock it with big game animals that were not native to the area, such as wild boar, sheep and mule deer, as well as native species like bear, turkey, pheasant and elk. The project, by most accounts, was an abysmal failure. By 1926 it was liquidated, with most of the animals either sold or dead, except for the wild boars that escaped and flourished in the surrounding wilderness.

These animals are almost indestructible, with huge, thick, heavily cartilaged shoulders; long, razor-sharp tusks; and hooves that they use to maim and kill anything in their path. Not only are these beasts dangerous, but they are also capable of inflicting tremendous amounts of property damage, rooting out crops in the fields, as well as destroying endangered native fauna. Yet, they possess a sort of dignified, almost arrogant, pride and are fiercely beautiful in their own curious way. Hog hunter John Jackson describes them as "the most regal animal I have ever seen."

Hunters and their Plott hounds throughout the mountain empire declared war on the beasts and hunted them with no regulations year-round from 1926 to 1936. They killed hundreds of them and lost scores of dogs to injury and death in the process. Yet the boars continued to thrive in their new home. They bred among themselves, and with local feral hogs, creating an almost invincible breed. The boar became even more dangerous to the Plott dogs than the meanest rogue bear.

The boar posed a new challenge for the Plott dogs and their owners, but one that they both welcomed. They quickly learned new tricks to combat these super hogs, and over the years many Plott hound owners would use and train a few of their dogs just for hog hunting and others just for bear hunting. Some, however, used the superb intelligence and skills of the breed to hunt both. But either way, the wild boar required the Plott hounds to hunt and fight in a somewhat different manner than they normally did when on the trail of bear and other native predators.

Striking a trail and staying on it was much the same for both, except the hog was even more evasive and unpredictable than the bear, more likely to zig-zag, circle and turn back to attack dogs and hunters. But like the bruin, the boar could run all day. However, unlike the bear, the hog could not climb a tree and hide, so unless it totally escaped, there would almost always be a bloody battle between boar and dog.

The smartest, healthiest and longest living Plott hounds learned early on not to physically fight a bear. The bruin is just too big and strong for the dog to win that battle. Old-time hunters admired the courage and grit of aggressive bear dogs, but preferred that they be "hair pullers" who would nip and bite at their prey—not latch onto it. By this they meant that if the dogs made a habit of latching onto or biting a bear, they were eventually going to be seriously hurt or killed. This term of latching, or holding, onto big game is also known as "catching" and is a term that is used primarily in hog hunting. But in bear hunting, the preferred method is to stay close to the bruin and contain, frustrate or "bay" it, while the hunter moves in and makes the kill.

This is where hog and bear hunting greatly differ. Since the primary danger to the dog is the sharp tusks of the boar, the best boar dogs quickly learned to stay away from them and attack the flanks or hind legs instead. Coming at them from this angle, they can latch or catch onto the ear of the hog. One to three skilled Plott dogs can control a hog in this manner until the hunter can make the kill, or tie the boar. The mistake many young or inexperienced dogs make is to attack the razorback from the front. It is a mistake they won't usually make but once. They will either be badly injured, and hopefully learn from it, or get killed if they don't.

The boar is not only dangerous to the dog, but to the hunter, too. Very few boar hunters can claim not to have had a run-in themselves with the wily boar. As West

Taylor Crockett's Lummox shown fighting a wild hog. Lummox was lucky here and survived attacking the hog head on. Ideally the attack is made from the rear or flanks of the hog.

Virginia bear hunter Sam George told me at APA Plott Days in 2007, "Any hog hunter who will tell you that a hog ain't never run him up a tree, is either lying or ain't hunted hogs very much."

Like Von Plott, Sam George's primary focus for big game hunting was, and is, bear. But he makes a good point. And no less a celebrated hunter than Von Plott himself was reluctant to put his Plott hounds on a boar trail, saying: "That is a quick way for a man to put himself right out of the dog business."

Von Plott's good friend, C.E. "Bud" Lyon, agrees with Von regarding hog hunting. Though he has successfully hunted hogs with such celebrated Plott dog legends as Taylor Crockett, Lyon says that he eventually gave up hog hunting with his Plotts because he simply "thought too much of his dogs, to put them at that much risk." Lyon added, "I don't mean to imply that hog hunters care any less for their dogs than I do. I am sure they do. But's it's just not something I want to do anymore."

Clearly, the wild boar brought a whole new dimension to big game hunting in the mountain empire. Because of this excitement, and the fact that the pork is pretty tasty too, it is somewhat ironic, but understandable, that many hunters then and now favor hunting the nonnative wild boar over the native king of the mountain empire—the black bear. But most equally enjoy and look forward to hunting them both, as do their Plott dogs.

Cable family patriarch, John Baker "Little John" Cable, a notable bear hunter, friend to Horace Kephart and proponent of the Cable Plott hound. Note the flintlock rifle that he used to hunt with all his life.

So now, with two types of big game roaming the Appalachain range, and thanks to a network of Plott hound families and their dogs scattered throughout the region, word of these wonderful canines gradually began to reach the outside world. Though the area was remote and still frontier-like in many ways, by the late 1800s outdoor writers had begun to come here to write of the exploits of the Plott dogs and of hunting and fishing in general. By the early 1900s, newspaper and magazine stories were common regarding this subject.

Horace Kephart wrote from Medlin, North Carolina, in an article for *Forest and Stream* magazine (October 28, 1905) of a week-long bear hunt he intended to go on the next day with "Little John" Cable and his Plott hounds, as well as some other Plott dogs and their owners from Waynesville, North Carolina. I assume Kephart was referring to Plott family members here, but cannot say for sure.

Kephart's mention of "Little John" Cable is a good place to start when reviewing some of the better-known local Plott hound owners in the network who helped perpetuate, and in some cases improve on, the Plott dog legacy. We already mentioned two of these notable families in the previous chapter—the Evans-Phillips family, whose Plott hounds would eventually evolve into today's Crockett-Plott dogs, as well as the Reece brothers and their lep dogs, both noteworthy examples of influences outside the Plott family. But the Cable and Blevins families would also play significant roles in the development of the Plott hound breed.

Like the Plotts, the Cables were early settlers in the Smokies. They moved from the Watauga Valley region of East Tennessee, south to Cades Cove in 1825. Later, in 1835, they were one of the first white families to settle in the Hazel Creek, North Carolina area. It was here that their reputation as Plott dog men and hunters quickly grew. John Baker Cable Jr., also known as "Little John," was one of the more famous members of the Cable family, along with his sons, Alphonso, Milburn and twins Jake and Hezikiah.

Little John hunted mostly with a muzzleloading gun, and like Amos Plott, once killed a bear with a knife, which in Little John's case he had made himself, as he was a fine blacksmith. Little John was also well known for following his dogs close and being the first person to get to the bear. His son Alphonso, who was also called "Fonz" or "Fawns" by Horace Kephart, was also famous for this trait.

Little John had received some dogs from the Plott family and from Plott family relatives—including the Monteith family of Cherokee County—in the late 1800s. Cable was pleased with the dogs and later began to breed them with other area hunting dogs to get the results he was seeking. As Michael Frome once wrote, "The back country hunter will breed his dogs and cross them until he produces the choice offspring that can run like a rabbit dog, trail like a foxhound, stay with the treed bear with the tenacity of a coon dog, and fight like the dickens until the bear or dog lies dead."

These dogs, though Plott in origin, became known as Cable hounds. They were usually a dark solid brindle color, with big, blocky, almost square-shaped heads, and were generally a bit bigger than a full-blooded Plott. They were celebrated among old-time hunters as being "stickers," meaning that they had the unique talent of staying on a game trail for extended periods of time. The Cable dogs were known to trail, tree and fight, if need be, for hours, even days at a time. This was probably one of the best-

Alphonzo "Fonz" Cable with a Cable Plott hound. Note the size and shape of head of this fine Cable family dog.

known traits of the Cable dogs. Two of them even became famous and received notice in *Ripley's Believe It or Not* magazine for these skills.

The Cable family was very religious and would not hunt on Sunday. Once while hunting they struck a bear trail on a Saturday afternoon, staying in hot pursuit of the bruin until late Saturday night. They soon realized that it was almost midnight and left their dogs on the hunt while they went home themselves to observe the Sabbath. They returned to the scene on Monday and found signs of where the dogs had treed and fought the bear numerous times, leaving a clear trail for the Cables to follow. This process had obviously continued for several more miles, with the Cables finding still more evidence of further fights and bear sign. After several hours of hard walking, they heard the barking of their exhausted dogs. The Cable boys eventually found their hounds with the same bear, up yet another tree, having trailed, bayed and fought it for over forty-eight hours.

Taylor Crockett got his first Plott hounds from Mont Plott's son Samuel, but he also admired and bred to Cable stock. He obtained these dogs from the Arrwood family, who were friends of the Cables. Crockett felt that the Cables—especially Jess, who later lived in Clay County, North Carolina—were the best puppy trainers who ever lived. He once took one of his pups, Old Wheeler, to Jess Cable to train. Crockett returned again some days later pleased to find Jess and Old Wheeler with a groundhog cornered in its den. Crockett asked how long his pup had been there, and Jess replied in a somewhat dejected tone of voice: "Only four hours." This was of course exceptional for any dog, as most hounds, especially pups, tired easily after twenty to forty-five minutes.

Some of the Cables were also skilled racoon hunters and sold the skins for profit. Like most bear or boar hunters, who used their Plott dogs exclusively for big game hunting, they would hunt their dogs on coons only after they had retired them from the big game arena. They had tremendous success using this method. The Cables once bragged that they had two of these dogs so well trained that they could keep a coon treed for days or even weeks at a time if need be. According to the Cables, once the dogs had a coon treed, one would rest, eat or sleep as needed, while the other remained vigilant at his post under the tree, thus enabling them to keep a coon at bay for indefinite periods of time. These were the two dogs that gained recognition from *Ripley's Believe It or Not*.

This could be yet another hunter tall tale, but it is an entertaining one, nevertheless.

Horace Kephart recalled in his book *Our Southern Highlanders* that the Cable dogs of Little John Cable were "as dangerous to man as well as to the brutes they were trained to fight; but Little John was their master and soon booted them into surly subjection." Kephart asked Cable if the Plott hounds were the best bear dogs in the mountains. Cable replied:

> *Tain't so, the Plott curs are the best: that is half hound, half cur, though what we-uns calls the cur, in this case really is a big furrin [foreign] dog that I don't rightly know the breed of. Feller's, you can talk as you please about a streak o' the cur spilin' [spoiling] a dog; but I know it hit ain't so—not for bear fightin' in these mountains, whar you cain't follow on horseback, but have to do your own running.*

Kephart then asked Cable what the reason was for this, to which he answered:

Well, hits like this: a plumb cur, of course can't follow a cold track, he just runs by sight, and he won't hang, he quits. But the other way, no hound will really fight a bear, hit takes a big severe dog to do that. Hounds has the best noses and they will run a bear all day, all night and the next day too; but they won't never tree—they are afraid to close in. Now look at them dogs of mine. My dogs can foller any trail, sames as a hound, but they will run right in on the varmint, a snappin' and clawin' and worryin' him 'til he gets so mad you can hear his tushes pop half a mile. He can't run away, he has to stop and fight, finally he gits tired and trees to rest hisself. Then we-uns catches up and finishes him!

These Cable dogs, like their Plott hound relatives, liked nothing better than to hunt. Nothing made them happier, and only the strongest of chains could keep them from the game trail. By the early 1900s, the lumber companies were cutting timber on and above Hazel Creek near the Cable homeplace. The companies ran their narrow-gauge Shay locomotives far back into the mountains to haul the logs out, taking empty flatbed log cars up the mountain and returning later with them full of timber.

It seems that the Cables had a beloved female bear dog that absolutely lived to hunt. However, as she had just had a litter of puppies, the Cable boys tied her up and left her at home with them, as they left to hunt instead with some of their other dogs. Several hours later, as the party headed deeper into "the back of beyond," they stopped to watch the lumber train as it toiled slowly up the mountain. As the train chugged past them, much to their surprise, they saw the prized female dog sitting proudly on one of the empty flatbed cars. She had somehow managed to free herself, but evidently soon realized the Cables had too big a lead on her to catch up. Instead, she hopped the train to make up for lost time. The love of the hunt overcame even the mother's natural love for her pups as she left them to follow the Cables on yet another game trail.

This may fall into yet another one of those proud dog owner stories, similar to that of the Cables' pal, Quill Rose. But even if only partially true, it nevertheless shows the gritty determination and intelligence of these fine canines. There is one thing, though, that we can never question or doubt—the Cable hounds were some of the finest bear dogs in the mountain empire network and a proud, vital part of Plott hound history.

The W.T. "Will" Orr family, whose descendants still run an inn catering to hunters near Robbinsville, North Carolina, also had their own well-known Plott hounds. They originally obtained their dogs through "the tow sack network" started by Mont Plott. The family eventually developed their own line of dogs, a predominantly black dog with brindle trim. Will Orr had many great dogs. One of his favorites was a "strike" dog named Jack, who was half Plott and half Redbone, a combination the Orrs favored. Jack was a fierce boar hunter until he was almost killed by a boar in the Swan Meadow area of the Smokies. The injury traumatized the dog so badly that upon his recovery he would never strike a boar trail again. But that was not the norm for the Orr hounds, as Will and his Plott pack killed seven boars in one month alone, November 1946.

The Orrs, like most mountaineers, considered their best hounds to be beloved members of their family. And woe be it to anyone who hurt either. It is said that Will Orr's brother Andy once killed a man who had intentionally shot one of his dogs. This in itself was not that unusual and something that a lot of old-time mountain families felt a person was justified in doing. A sort of Old Testament "eye for an eye" code of honor often prevailed in the Smokies and is further proof of the esteemed value these folks placed on their dogs.

The Blevins clan is yet another distinguished family in Plott hound history, one whose influence began first in Yancey and Mitchell Counties, North Carolina, in the late 1800s, and later spread across the mountain empire, eventually reaching Graham County, North Carolina, by the 1920s. Some say that the Blevins-Plott connection started like most, with Montraville Plott, who in about 1890 gave the Blevinses some Plott pups. The Blevinses, like many other mountaineers, already had fine dogs of their own. But they were even more pleased when they bred them with the Plott hounds. The Blevinses would return to Plott Valley yearly for two decades, continuing to refine their own stock.

Soon these dogs became known as Blevins hounds. They developed a reputation as superb big game dogs known for their melodious voice and keen nose. The Blevins-Plott hound was a brindled black and coal, with a black saddle. (A black saddle almost always occurs when a brindle dog is crossed with a high tan dog.) The Blevins hounds had shorter ears and had no "pumpkin seeds" above their eyes like modern-day black-and-tan hounds. They were known especially for being fast trailers and feisty fighters that would run to catch a bear. There was simply no "back up" in these dogs.

The Blevins family, while living in the area in and around Mitchell and Yancey Counties, were friends with yet another celebrated mountain family, the Wilsons. The Wilsons used Blevins dogs, too, among others, and were arguably the most prominent bear hunters and trappers ever to live in a state that was known for them. By the early 1900s Blaine Blevins was living on the confluence of Little Snowbird and Big Snowbird Creeks in Graham County. It was here that the Blevins hound strain of Plott dog would become famous. It was also where they would eventually intermarry with yet another skilled family of hunters and dog men—the Birchfields. The entire Birchfield family, particularly Nathan and Sam, were well known as fine hunters.

But the Blevins hound and Blevins family's biggest claim to fame in Plott dog history is the role they played in the birth and development of two of the most exceptional Plott hounds who ever lived, the legendary Boss and Tige. These prestigious Plott dogs, bred in the 1920s by Gola Ferguson, quickly achieved national fame. Most of the originally registered Plott hounds can be traced back to these two distinguished dogs. We will discuss them in-depth in the next chapter.

Another interesting, but little known, contributor to Plott hound history are members of the Cherokee Nation. These area natives lived both on the reservation, or Qualla Boundary, as well as scattered throughout the mountain empire, particularly in the Snowbird Mountain range, where some of the more traditional Cherokee families made their home. The Cherokee had some fine specimens of old-time Plott hounds. But, like the Plott family themselves, most of the tribal members who possessed them were pretty tight-lipped as to their origins.

Taylor Crockett's Suzi Q. A Crockett-Plott with strong Blevins family influences.

The best example of a descendant of the old-time Cherokee Plott hound came later in 1946 from Rickey Red Eagle, who was one of the first people to officially register his Plott hounds. Most Cherokees say that they bought or traded for their Plotts from neighbors or friends—most likely some of the celebrated hunters and families mentioned in this chapter—and that they were passed down through their families, generation to generation, just like the Plotts. The Cherokee people, too, deserve credit for maintaining and preserving fine examples of the old-time, raw-boned, aggressive, athletic and intelligent Plott hound.

By the late 1920s, a network of elite Plott hound hunters and breeders had spread across a vast mountain empire that stretched throughout the southern Appalachians, led by the Plott, Phillips, Evans, Cheek, Cable, Blevins, Wilson, Reece, Arrwood and Orr families, all of whom played a part in laying the foundation for what I call "the golden age" of Plott hound history. This was when the "Big Five"—consisting of brothers Von and John A. Plott, along with Gola Ferguson, Isaiah Kidd and Taylor Crockett—burst onto the national scene, finally bringing the Plott hound the worldwide fame and recognition that it so richly deserved.

Chapter Eight

THE BIG FIVE

There will always be arguments and debates as to whose Plott dogs were best, who the best breeders and hunters were and who has done the most to preserve the legacy of the Plott dogs. But few will argue that it was the "Big Five" who had the largest impact on what we now refer to as the modern-day Plott hound. When discussing the Big Five there is no better place to start than with the Plott brothers, John and Vaughn.

JOHN AND VAUGHN PLOTT

John A. Plott, the oldest son of Montraville and Julia Plott, and his youngest brother, Henry Vaughn "Von" Plott, like their father and forefathers before them, were avid hunters and master dog breeders. Both were fiercely dedicated to advancing, yet maintaining, the original Plott hound. However, like a lot of brothers, their ideas on the best way to do this differed greatly, as did their opinions on other things as well.

Even in their appearance and demeanor the Plott brothers were as different as night and day. The older John was more reserved, taciturn and dignified, while the younger brother, Von, was a rowdy sort of fellow, always looking for fun, though he could at times be curt and short tempered. Both were strong, handsome men, but yet again, in very different ways. John, even in the woods, looked the part of a distinguished businessman or elder statesman, and Von looked more like a rugged cowboy from a Saturday matinee western.

Many experts feel that John was more committed to keeping the Plott dog bloodlines as pure as possible, with only select outside infusions allowed. Some feel that John, like his father Mont before him, disliked the idea of his dogs being called hounds or of them having hound genes in their lineage. Von was also deeply committed to promoting Plott hounds, but he seemed to be mostly focused on results, and sometimes more open to considering the adding of other dogs to the family lineage—dogs that he felt would be advantageous both for him to hunt with, as well as to improve Plott hound bloodlines. Both brothers quickly mastered their family's superb animal husbandry skills. Von

John A. Plott in 1938 with a fine brindle Plott hound.

Von Plott with notable Plott dogs (left to right): Plott's Happy, Plott's Balsam and Plott's Link.

Von Plott and Jake Nichols with famous Plott hounds (left to right): Plott's Jenny, Plott's Link, Bill's Bell, Plott's Drum, Plott's Happy, Plott's Balsam, Plott's John and Plott's Roxie. Happy and Roxie were parents to the great Von Plott strike dog Blue Boy.

was better than most in that regard, as he was often able to hide the more distinct bloodhound traits found in his later dogs.

John supposedly once said that Von's dogs had made too many trips to the prison camp. Many folks thought that this perhaps was John's way of making the accusation that Von's dogs were more "houndy" in a somewhat humorous manner. I don't believe this was entirely the case, and instead think that that was literally what John meant. There was, and still is, a prison camp near Plott Valley in Hazelwood, North Carolina, and in an interview with the *Foxfire* staff in about 1976, Von stated that he had indeed worked there as a prison guard for several years. So it is entirely possible that Von bred some of his dogs with bloodhounds while he was employed there. But either way, he definitely had easy breeding access to them if he wished to do so.

Regardless of how it originally happened, Von's later dogs most definitely had a more "houndy" appearance than John's dogs. Generally they were much bigger, with looser skin and longer ears, but had the same brindle coats. There are ample photos to verify this, and one of Von's most famous dogs, Plott's Lady Belle, is a prime example of it, as were Plott's Jenny, Plott's Balsam Rock and Plott's Ruby.

Yet if you look at some of Von's earlier dogs, many still retained the look of the old-time Plott hounds. Some prime examples of these dogs were Plott's Scott, his brother Plott's Dan, Bute, Buck, Fannie, Queen, Mike and Jake, all of whom were on the 1935 Branch Rickey bear hunt. Other examples include Plott's Hobo and his father Plott's Mack and mother Plott's Flirt, as well as the buckskin dog, Plott's Little Man, and his sire Haywood Red and dam Plott's Lady. (Little Man was killed by a bear called "Ole Bigfoot" while on a hunt in coastal North Carolina.) It was in the late 1940s to early 1960s that the more hound-like influences that Von later favored became more prominent in his dogs.

While John and Mont disliked any connection of the Plott breed with hounds, Von just as strongly detested the leopard dog cross that Mont had done with Elijah Crow in 1884. He vowed that his dogs would never again have any of those bloodlines. Von even went as far as making anyone who obtained dogs from him promise that they would never breed any leopard dogs with his stock. John did not share this belief, and as we will soon see, he later infused more leopard blood into his dogs, as did his brother "Big" George.

Before proceeding further I want to emphasize that I am not saying John's commitment to his family's dogs was any better or stronger than Von's. Nor am I saying that Von cared nothing for the legacy and heritage of the Plott dogs. I think that he did. But I do believe, as do most recognized dog experts, that while both John and Von Plott were deeply committed to the best future interests of the Plott hound, their methods and approach to achieving this objective were decidedly different. And there is nothing wrong with that. One brother preferred one type of Plott dog while the other brother liked another strain. But the end result is an argument that will be debated by Plott hound enthusiasts forever.

Plott dog purists will argue that Von's primary objective was to continually refine and improve Plott bloodlines, seeking to develop the perfect big game hunting dog, but that in doing so he bred out some of the intelligence and multipurpose skills of the old-time dogs. Or, as John Jackson describes it in the 2006 *APA Brindle Book*, "In some ways it is disheartening to know that in our rush to create the slobber mouthed, track-driving Plott HOUND, we have nearly bred the protoype and original [dog] into obscurity."

Still other experts will insist that Von was doing nothing differently than the Plott family had done for hundreds of years, dating back to their days in Germany—that is constantly tinkering with and refining breeding infusions to achieve the dog best suited for their respective needs. In reality, he was simply doing whatever he thought he needed to do to get the most bear kills. The end results were all that really mattered to Von. And, many will add that this makes Von a true purist or traditionalist himself.

Both factions make very valid points, and this is a subject that will be endlessly debated for as long as there are Plott hounds. But one thing is for sure, John and Von both felt strongly about whose dogs were best, and for that reason, as well as perhaps others, the brothers both stubbornly refused to have much to do with each other throughout their lifetimes. That is, until shortly before John's death in 1959, when they finally made their peace. Even then, their opinions on whose dogs were best remained markedly different.

Von Plott at age twenty-four in 1920, about the same time that Montraville Plott turned over his last Plott hounds to him. Dogs pictured are (left to right) Jake, Maude and Boss.

Von stated in several magazines and books that when his father Mont no longer was able to hunt, in about 1917 or 1918, he turned over full responsibility and ownership of the entire Plott dog pack to him. Both John and Ellis Plott were living out west then, so it appears that Von, though very well qualified, was simply in the right place at the right time to inherit the pack. But considering the fame and recognition that Von Plott would bring to the breed for more than the next half a century, Mont clearly made the right choice.

Nevertheless, no matter what the reason, by 1920 Von was indeed the sole owner of a Plott dog pack that had been in his family for almost 175 years. Over the years, many have portrayed this as a large acquisition of a lot of dogs. But the truth is, according to Von himself, Mont had only five dogs at the time of his death. It is an ironic and interesting coincidence that this was the same number of hounds that Johannes had originally brought to America in 1750. Von, of course, already had many dogs of his own—just how many, no one knows for sure. But his own dogs, combined with the five hounds he acquired from Mont, left Von with a formidable pack of outstanding Plott hounds, although his brother John would certainly not agree with this assessment.

It was also around 1920 that John Plott and his young family returned to Plott Valley to resume their lives farming and raising prized livestock. This, too, was when

John A. Plott homeplace in Plott Valley, outside of Waynesville, North Carolina. This was the site of the original Henry Plott homestead, dating back to 1800.

John got back into the dog business. John Plott told Dale Brandenburger, of Pioneer Kennel fame, that by the time he returned home he felt that the Plott pack had "gone down a lot" and was well below his usual standards. He was disheartened by this, and he immediately set out to get his own pack started again, a pack that would be based on the early standards set by his father. Due to the network of Plott dogs and owners spread across the mountain empire, it was still fairly easy to find pure Plott hound stock. It wasn't long before John had a dog pack of his own that would rival that of his brother Von or anyone else in the region.

Maybe John got some of these dogs from Von Plott or his other brothers. Maybe he searched the mountains, perhaps visiting the Phillips or Evans families for some of that old-time Mont Plott stock that was scattered throughout the hills. No one knows for sure. We do know that in a relatively short period of time John had restored the pack to the standards he desired, and he had begun to share his knowledge and love for dogs and hunting with his beloved son, "Little" George.

By the 1930s, we also know that John and his son had secured some old-time stock from other mountain families, as well as from Rolen Owens, a friend of John's who he had once worked with in a Transylvania County, North Carolina Civilian Conservation Corps camp. Owens had some old-time stock that still retained the lep bloodlines that Mont Plott had first brought into the line in 1884. Owens had mated a one-eighth lep to a full-blooded brindle Plott with excellent results. Though, as noted in Chapter Five, Mont disliked the lep dogs and eventually culled them from his pack, John felt differently about this issue and mated some of the Owens stock to his own. This union resulted in seven pups, four of them leopard brindle, three of which John

John Plott and Ed Lambert with prime examples of true old-time Plott hounds. Blue Joe and Lep are the third and fourth dogs from the left.

and Little George, who was now a young man, kept for themselves. Two of these pups would achieve legendary status in the Plott dog world. They were registered as John Plott's Lep and Smithdeal's Blue Joe. Most agree that Plott's Lep was one of John Plott's all-time favorite dogs. These dogs, and their descendants in years to come, would greatly impact modern-day Plott hound history.

Both Plott brothers now had superb dogs, yet continued to spend their adult lives at odds with each other. There was, however, one bridge between them that remained constant and true. This was John's son, Little George, who clearly was the apple of his father's eye. They were extremely close, yet Little George managed to also maintain a quality relationship with his Uncle Von. Strangely enough, it was a relationship that never seemed to interfere with the bond between he and his father. Little George and Von enjoyed many hunting trips and adventures together until George entered the military during World War II. Little George shared the devotion both men had for the Plott breed and their love for the hunt. He seemed to provide a sort of balance between the two brothers, understanding and relating to what both wanted for the future of their dogs.

Because of his reserved nature we don't know a lot of details regarding John's lifetime exploits. But by the start of World War II, he and his son apparently had a fine pack of

John A. Plott and a leopard-colored Plott hound.

Little George Plott with Oliver Laws and Taylor Wilson and classic examples of old-time Plott dogs. Note the uniformity of these beautiful hounds.

Plott hounds. As a result, between he and Von's dogs, along with those owned by their other brothers and the other families in the Plott dog network, the breed was stronger than ever.

It was in the years leading up to and during the war that the Plott hound was officially "discovered" and began to gain nationwide fame. For years news stories had gradually begun to make people who lived outside the mountains aware of the exploits of the Plott dogs. But it was in 1935, when Little George and Von were contracted to take St. Louis Cardinal baseball team executive Branch Rickey on a bear hunt, that the Plott hounds' fame was forever guaranteed.

Branch Rickey, a professional baseball Hall of Fame member, best known for the role he played in integrating professional baseball with the signing of Jackie Robinson, was also an avid bear hunter. He probably had read of the Plott family and their dogs in some of Raymond Camp's *New York Times* articles, or perhaps in some other national publications. But, at any rate, Rickey apparently contracted Von and Little George Plott in the fall of 1935 to guide him on a bear hunt in the Hazel Creek area of the Smokies.

Rickey, along with Von and Little George Plott, who were joined by their friends Jim Laws, Bob Haynes, Oliver Laws, Taylor Wilson and several others, set off on what would turn out to be a record setting hunt. Several famous Plott hounds, such as Plott's

Von Plott and Branch Rickey on 1935 hunt.

Scott, Plott's Dan, Bute, Buck, Fannie, Queen, Mike, Jake, Lady, Kate, Drum, Mack, Sunshine, Stroll, Bess, Betty and Hardwood, all participated in this historical hunt.

Their party jumped twenty bears in three days and killed eight, six in one day, a record that still stands today. These dogs, of which we have plenty of photos, are some of the best examples of early Plott hounds on record, and remain admired and loved throughout the Plott hound world. In fact, many consider the Plott hounds Dan and Bess to be the finest examples of Von Plott linebreeding on record. They were supposedly the best two bear dogs in the legendary lineup of hounds that participated in this historical hunt.

On December 5, 1935, Branch Rickey wrote Von Plott a letter regarding the hunt. Rickey opened the letter by referring to himself as a "tenderfoot hunter" and telling Von how much he enjoyed their hunt. He goes on to praise the fine Plott hounds on the hunt, especially Scotty and Drum. Rickey then commends Von on his hunting skills, writing in part:

> *I shall never forget your ability to run as fast as those dogs, or just about as fast; and particularly shall I never forget that when I had that wounded bear down by the creek with Scotty fighting him in and out and you were the first to arrive…*
>
> *Everyone agrees that you ran more than twelve miles that morning up and down those mountains; and at every crossing and across every hillcrest you were never seen to be walking—you were always running. You are what I call a finished hunter. And I think I would rather go hunting with you in charge of the dogs than anyone else in the world.*

1935 Branch Rickey bear hunt near Hazel Creek, North Carolina. Rickey is third from right and Von Plott second from right. Dogs were Plott's Scott and Dan, Bute, Buck, Fannie, Queen, Mike, Jake, Lady, Kate, Drum, Mack, Sunshine, Stroll, Bess, Betty and Hardwood.

That's a pretty strong compliment from a man who had the means to hunt anywhere, anytime and with anyone he wished. Rickey's comments only further verify Von Plott's legendary status in Plott hound history. In closing his letter, Rickey added what would eventually prove to be a poignant comment regarding Little George Plott: "Please give my best regards to George. He is a fine boy, and ought to make his mark in the world at something or other. Indeed, I think he will in whatever he undertakes."

John Jackson wrote that this hunt was yet another example of the key role Little George played in Plott hound history. Along with the numerous hunting adventures he shared with the elder Plotts, Little George was also present when Tennessee businessman Hack Smithdeal officially played his role in the "national discovery" of the Plott dog in the early 1940s. Smithdeal, an enthusiastic bear hunter and prominent businessman, was looking to buy the best bear dogs around. He first contacted Ewart Wilson in an effort to buy his dogs. Wilson refused, but he invited Smithdeal on a bear hunt where he first met Von and Little George Plott and a truck full of their brindled Plott bear hounds.

Even then, Smithdeal astutely observed how the Plott hounds of Little George and Von differed somewhat from each other in manner and appearance. He noted that Little George's dogs were "a fast, closer fighting, quick and agile dog," whereas Von's were "a more houndy, colder nosed variety, more adept at trailing." The Plott dogs all performed magnificently on the hunt. Smithdeal had to have them. Like many before him, and after, he had immediately contracted a severe case of "Plott hound fever." He was "bitten" so badly, in fact, that he borrowed the money to buy the entire pack right then and there. Smithdeal purchased every dog that Von and George had brought with them, and returned with the hounds to his home in Johnson City, Tennessee. This was the start of a longtime relationship between Smithdeal and the Plott family, and the Plott hound's first big step toward true national recognition.

As World War II raged on, Little George, like many other young American patriots of the era, including my late father, joined the army to defend his country. While stationed in Fort Carson, Colorado, in 1944, Little George contacted Hack Smithdeal by phone and arranged to sell his part of his father's (John Plott) pack to him. This purchase would help make Smithdeal famous in the Plott hound world, as one of these dogs was the celebrated Blue Joe. Little George left the next day for service overseas in the European Theatre.

Perhaps it was his own premonition of impending doom. Or maybe it was that he could not stand the idea of his beloved dogs not being able to hunt in his absence. Maybe it was nothing more than a young man far away from home needing some spending money—but we will never know the real reasons that Little George sold his beloved dogs to Hack Smithdeal. He was killed shortly after the transaction, on Christmas Eve, 1944, while crossing the English Channel aboard the troop carrier, the SS *Leopoldville*. This was indeed a tragedy, but later proved to be even more so when it was learned that his death perhaps could have been avoided.

The *Leopoldville*, with over 1,700 troops aboard and only five miles from its destination, was torpedoed by a German U-boat. About 300 troops were killed instantly, but the captain radioed for help to transfer the remaining survivors to safety before his ship sank. After several hours of waiting, a British destroyer finally arrived and was able to rescue 500 men. But due to high seas and military red tape, the remaining troops were left for hours to wait for help that would never come. The *Leopoldville* slowly sank, and 1,000 men were eventually forced to evacuate into the ice cold waters of the English Channel. Of those 1,000, 763 of them died, and 493 of their bodies were never recovered, including the body of Captain Little George Plott.

John Plott by all accounts never fully recovered from the death of his only son. Fortunately, he died in 1959 without ever learning of the military fiasco, which, if avoided, perhaps could have saved his son's life. Taylor Crockett's father was the minister that presided over John Plott's funeral service. Taylor recalled that his father thought very highly of Plott and considered John to have been an extremely honest man of the utmost integrity.

John Plott kept Plott dogs the remainder of his life to honor Little George and to carry the family torch. But his heart was never truly in it again. Perhaps he took some solace in knowing that he had remained true to his father's wishes and had done his very best to preserve the legacy of the early old-time multipurpose Plott hounds that Plott purists still admire and appreciate today. I certainly hope so.

The death of any child is tragic to their parents, relatives and friends. But the death of Little George Plott was especially tragic to the Plott hound world because we are left to wonder what amazing contributions he could have made to the breed and the sport of big game hunting in general had he survived. Lawrence Plott told Plott family friend

Clyde Neader that there was little doubt that the Plott hound of today would have been different had Little George lived to carry on the old-time traditional Plott dogs once favored by his grandpa Mont. Most experts agree that had he lived, the title of the Big Five would had to have been changed to the Big Six, as Little George Plott's name would surely have been added to that elite group.

Von Plott, while also greatly devastated by the loss of his nephew, nevertheless plunged forward, spending the rest of his life hunting all over the country and continuing to breed superb Plott hounds and farm animals. In addition to his other stock, Von raised fighting roosters, or gamecocks, and became well known throughout the South as a top-notch "cockfighter." The story goes that Von traded one of his more famous Plott hounds, Plott's Dan, to George Todd for some of Todd's prime gamecocks—and won many matches with them.

He also farmed, served as a hunting guide, worked as a prison camp guard and even did some fence work for a while in eastern North Carolina. But breeding and hunting Plott hounds was his true passion as he told the *Foxfire* folks in 1976. Recalling his earlier days, Von said that his father Mont seldom sold dogs and mostly gave them away to friends and neighbors. But he added that Mont did sell his first dog in about 1915 or 1916. According to Von, he did not sell dogs regularly himself until about 1932 or 1933, and he continued to sell a few dogs in 1976. Von said, "Our average selling price now is $75 to $150, but if you keep them a little longer you can get more for them. People raise them all over now, I have seen some cost anywhere from a thousand dollars up." Von Plott's son, the late Bill Plott, added, "If my Daddy kind of likes your looks, he might give you a dog, but if he don't like your looks he would not sell you a dog for any damn price."

Bill also recalled a prime example of the short temper that Von could sometimes exhibit. A preacher once visited their home looking over Von's dogs and observed that he liked most of them except for one. Bill said, "Daddy's worse to cuss than I am, of course he is older than me, so he's supposed to be worse. But Daddy replied to that preacher, 'I don't give a God damn whether you like him or not, I'm feeding him, and you can get the hell out of here now!'"

Henry Vaughn "Von" Plott died at the age of eighty-two in 1979, having led a rich and full life. It was a life that was every bit as memorable and colorful as that of his father Montraville's before him, or that of any other mountain legend or character such as Quill Rose, Little John Cable or Mark Cathey. More importantly, he lived to see his family's dogs gain national and international recognition, and he died knowing the integral part he had played in making that happen, thereby ensuring that the Plott hound legacy would continue.

Von and John Plott's brothers, Big George and Samuel, also stayed involved in the dog business, but never to the extent of their more celebrated brothers. Big George, like his nephew Little George, was a World War II veteran, who favored the lep dogs that Von so vehemently disliked. Later in his life Big George supplied dogs for some notable Michigan bear hunts, and he also bred the well-known Plott hound named Plott's Rube.

Samuel Plott was considered the family historian, and he was fiercely proud of his family and their dogs. His son Larry would carry on his tradition of preserving Plott

Von Plott dog in 1971.

Von Plott dog in 1971.

Plott brothers, hounds and friends on a bear hunt. Von Plott is on the far left, John A. Plott is second from left and Samuel Ellis Plott is bending on right.

history. One of Sam's dogs, Great Smoky, was an original registered Plott. Like Big George, Sam kept dogs, but he did not enjoy big game hunting as much as Von and John did. But make no mistake about it, Samuel Plott had some fine dogs too, and in fact, he would sell Taylor Crockett his first two Plott hounds. Samuel and his family eventually permanently moved to Chatsworth, Georgia.

To the best of my knowledge, Robert Ellis Plott chose to stay out west and never moved permanently back to Plott Valley, as his older brother John did in 1920. Ellis did come home to visit from time to time and is pictured on a few hunts, but he lived the remainder of his life in Texas. It is not known if he kept any dogs there or not.

So as far as membership in the elite Big Five, John and Von Plott are the only Plott family members who made the cut, though Little George Plott almost certainly would have joined them had he not been killed in World War II. However, cousin Herbert "Hub" Plott of Maggie Valley, North Carolina, also bears honorable mention among Plott family members, as he hunted and raised many great dogs during his lifetime. Hub, like his cousin Samuel, enjoyed Plott family history, and he shared a close bond with another member of the Big Five, Gola Ferguson. Hub often hunted with the McGha family, another widely known North Carolina bear hunting clan who raised Plott hounds. Herbert was the son of Robert Henry Plott. He seemed to recognize the distinguishing qualities of both Von and John Plott's dogs, as well as those of his good friend Gola Ferguson. As a result, Hub's dogs were more of a hound-cur blend or mix, perhaps his attempt in capturing the best qualities of both types of dog.

The next two members of the Big Five were lifelong friends of the Plott family, who grew up and lived near Plott Valley most of their lives. They are Gola Ferguson and H.T. Crockett.

GOLA FERGUSON

Gola Ferguson personified the definition of a true renaissance man. It is a term that is often overused in attempting to describe individuals who are experts in mulitple fields, but in Gola Ferguson's case, it describes him perfectly. He stands out in a generation of talented folks who believed they could do almost anything well—and often did.

Ferguson was born on June 28, 1887, near Kirkland Creek, outside of Bryson City, North Carolina. Like many farming families of that era, the Fergusons took their cattle to mountaintop pastures known as "balds" to graze there for the summer. Family members, usually teenage sons, would camp there, guarding the livestock as they fattened up for the winter. It was on these balds that Ferguson developed his love for hunting and began to learn animal husbandry skills.

Gola decided that he wanted to attend college, and he raised money for his tuition to Western Carolina University by selling and buying sheep. Ferguson, an exceptionally good-humored man, referred to himself as a "sheep broker." While in college, he met and married Jerdie Watson, and they moved to Dillsboro, North Carolina. After the birth of their first child, they moved to Bryson City. It was here that two more children were born and where his colorful career began. Gola farmed and taught school, eventually becoming a school principal, and he served as Swain County treasurer. He was elected sheriff of the county in 1926. His wife would also serve as his jailer. Over the remainder of his career he was also a surveyor, housebuilder, drew up deeds and became an accomplished luthier, building fifteen to twenty violins. Ferguson ran for Congress in 1942, and he was renowned as a colorful and entertaining storyteller and public speaker.

As impressive as all these achievements were, it was Ferguson's development of his own type of Plott hound that would bring him national fame and recognition. Gola lived near the Plott family his entire life. They were all close friends and had bred their dogs back and forth between their families over several decades. Ferguson acknowledged that he had obtained some of his original stock from the Plott family, most likely Mont Plott, in the early 1900s. He also obtained some original stock from both the Cable and Blevins families.

Like most old-time hunters and breeders, Gola firmly believed in the survival of the fittest. Breed the best to the best, get the results you want and cull the rest. Ferguson, on average, always had a pack of twenty to thirty top Plott hounds in his possession throughout his lifetime. By the early 1920s he had begun to get the results he was looking for. Ferguson's dogs were well known for their deep brownish brindle color and black saddlebacks, as well as for their keen intelligence and superb fighting skills. Like most

Plott dogs, the Ferguson-Plotts also were very comfortable in water, swimming streams with skills comparable to the best spaniels, labs or other exceptional water dogs.

The Ferguson-Plott hounds quickly became the favorite choice of many area bear hunters. Over the course of his hunting career, Gola would kill close to sixty bears using these fine animals. In 1927, while on a bear hunt, a friend suggested to him that perhaps he should try using his Ferguson-Plotts on wild boar hunts. Ferguson took his advice and eventually killed seventeen wild boars with his dogs, thus ensuring their reputation as great all-around big game hunting dogs.

Ferguson's two most famous dogs, indeed probably the two most renowned Plott dogs of any kind, were the legendary Boss and Tige. As with most canine legends, their specific origin or bloodline is often debated. Based on numerous interviews and research, I believe the following to be the most accurate account of their lineage.

In the 1920s there was a country doctor living in Haywood County named Joshua Fanning Able. Doctor Able loved to hunt bear and owned a large black canine that had gained regional notoriety as an exceptional hunting dog. Evidently, Able had developed a pack of his own dogs, based around this fine animal, and in some circles they were known as "Able hounds."

No one knows for sure the exact genetic makeup of the Able hounds, particularly that of the favored large, black Able dog. But, we can say with some degree of certainty that Gola Ferguson bred this Able dog with a Plott hound and a Blevins dog to get Boss and Tige. The specific bloodlines for Boss and Tige could be one-fourth Plott with one-fourth Blevins and one-half Able. Or, more likely, the bloodlines consisted of one-half Plott hound, one-fourth Blevins dog and one-fourth Able dog lineage.

Boss was a large, heavy-boned saddleback, almost three times bigger than Tige. Tige was a smaller, gray-brindled dog. Taylor Crockett said that Tige favored the old-time cur, while Boss was more hound-like in appearance. Gola Ferguson said these animals were two of the best "strike" dogs that he ever owned and referred to Boss and Tige as "his five-star generals." He noted, too, that both Boss and Tige were absolutely fearless, yet were so intelligent that they almost always avoided serious injury while in combat with big game. Of the nearly one hundred Plott hounds originally registered in 1946 with the United Kennel Club, eighty or more of them originated from these two amazing dogs, Boss and Tige.

But it was yet another of Ferguson's pack that he felt was his all-time best dog. This dog, whose name was Jap, was nearly completely black, with brindle legs, medium ears and unusual reddish-colored eyes. When it came to bear hunting, Gola described Jap as a "one-man army." Taylor Crockett handled Jap for Ferguson on some of his earliest hunts. Crockett recalled that Jap looked a lot like the later Plott's Hobo and weighed about sixty pounds. The legendary Plott hound Pistol Packing Mama was also sired by Jap, and was later owned by Von Plott. Pistol Packing Mama would also produce another great Plott hound, Plott's Punie, a fast, long-legged hound that proved to be a fine bear dog. Other acclaimed Ferguson Plott hounds include his "strike" dog Spinner, Ferguson's Lad, and Ferguson's Mark—the pup of Ferguson's Diesel and Ferguson's Meter.

For the remainder of his life Gola Ferguson continued to be an expert hunter, as well as an incredibly talented dog breeder. Like Isaiah Kidd, Gola, with the help of his wife

Gola Ferguson with his esteemed dog Jap, who he referred to as "a one-man army" while hunting bear.

Pistol Packing Mama, one of Gola Ferguson's all-time best Plotts, who was later owned by Von Plott.

Jerdie, kept exceptional breeding records, and they did things as scientifically as possible. It was Ferguson who once observed, "If you can dip far enough into the gene plasma, with luck, you can get the same traits of the old-time 200 year old dog."

Gola was always very close friends with the other members of the Big Five, but he was especially close to Taylor Crockett and Von Plott. Taylor Crockett often served as Ferguson's chief dog handler and observed that he was very easy to get along with and always kept his friends laughing with his jokes and stories. Crockett was quoted as saying that the noted humorist Will Rogers "couldn't hold a candle to Gola Ferguson."

Ferguson was also exceptionally close to Hub Plott, and he requested that Hub be given part of his dog pack when he died. Modern-day Plott legends Sam George, Bud Lyon and Robert Jones, among others, retain some of this stock today.

Gola Ferguson died at the age of seventy-five in 1962. The *New Dog Encylopedia* officially recognized him in 1970 for his contributions to dog breeding and big game hunting. Many dog experts feel that without the assistance of Gola Ferguson there would be no modern-day Plott hound. Like the Plott brothers, he left a rich legacy of a life

Mark and Belle, two superb Ferguson-Plott hounds.

well lived—and as a modern-day renaissance man who made enormous contributions to Plott hound history and the preservation of the breed.

HOWE TAYLOR CROCKETT

Howe Taylor Crockett was the youngest, and one of the more colorful and charismatic members of the Big Five. He was born the son of a Presbyterian minister on August 4, 1908, in Stoney Point, Tennessee. His family later moved to Kentucky until the end of World War I, and then moved to Black Mountain, North Carolina. Shortly after that the Crocketts relocated to Waynesville, North Carolina, when Taylor was still a child. It was here that he would become friends with the Plott family and first learn of the Plott hound. He would obtain his first two Plott hounds from Samuel Plott in Plott Valley in 1924.

From an early age Crockett loved the outdoors and the southern mountains. He quickly developed into an outstanding athlete and hunter. Taylor was a fine boxer and football lineman who played college football for what is now Brevard College, but was

Three famous Plott hounds with Von Plott and Gola Ferguson bloodlines—Carolina Kate, Plott's Belle and Pistol Packing Mama.

then known as Weaver College. As much as he loved organized sports, he loved bear hunting even more. Crockett told his friend John Jackson that he once broke curfew the night before a game to go on a bear hunt. Unfortunately, his coach caught him as he attempted to sneak back in his dorm, and he was benched for the game. Crockett later incorporated an aspect of his gridiron days into bear hunting, as he sometimes wore his football cleats for better traction while trailing his Plott dogs through harsh, mountainous terrain.

After leaving school, Crockett continued to keenly hunt bear and boar and tried various types of hunting dogs in his pursuits, including Plott hounds. He also earned a living working as a logger in one of the region's notoriously rugged logging camps. Thanks to his past athletic endeavors, combined with his logging career and regular strenuous hunts, Crockett developed extraordinary strength and stamina. He had massively broad shoulders and huge hands. His nose was crooked from being broken in boxing and logging mishaps. He was legendary for his ability to run nonstop for hours at a time, following his dogs through the steep laurel thickets on bear or boar trails. Taylor Crockett had grown into a strong and formidable man.

By the start of World War II, Taylor Crockett already had a great pack of hunting dogs with bloodlines from the Plott, Cable and Martin families. Two of these dogs were in on fifty-six boar kills in one hunting season shortly before Crockett was drafted into military service. It was during that same season that Crockett would first become impressed with the old-time Evans/Phillips Plott hounds. He vowed that if he made it back from the war he would have some of these dogs of his own.

Crockett was thirty-three years old when Pearl Harbor was attacked, but he was still drafted into the army to defend his country. He was on the same train leaving

Gola Ferguson and son Bart with their Ferguson-Plotts.

Waynesville for army training as Big George Plott, who was also a veteran of the conflict. Crockett was a highly decorated soldier, who saw extensive combat in North Africa, Sicily and Italy. He was twice seriously wounded and earned two Purple Hearts for his meritorious service.

Upon his return to the mountains after the war, Crockett fulfilled his promise of getting some Phillips/Evans Plott dogs. These hounds, combined with his earlier Plott dogs, would be the foundation of the celebrated Crockett-Plott dogs. But it was later when he obtained three pups from Paul Cheek that Crockett hit the dog breeding jackpot. These dogs were five-eighths Phillips/Evans stock and three-eights Cable hound. One of these would become one of Crockett's most famous dogs—the legendary Leo. It was Leo who would perhaps best epitomize the true old-time Plott dog. He was an exceptional farming and herding hound as he was gentle with small animals, yet he was a notably fierce fighting bear and boar dog. Leo and the rest of these dogs, combined with Crockett's earlier stock, resulted in a superstar old-time Plott hound line.

These Crockett-Plotts had no "houndy" traits at all. They had big, broad heads, with high-set, relatively short ears that possessed slight erectile capabilities. These canines were known for their wide, thick chests and muscular, athletic bodies. Their legs were medium in length, and they had a slightly flagged short-haired tail. They generally had light brindle coats and sometimes had white markings on their toes and chests.

The Crockett dogs were known to be ferocious, aggressive fighters noted for their grit and tenacity. They had a chop mouth—a short, staccato-type bark. No long, drawn-out howls for these hounds. They were notoriously protective of their owners and generally were gentle with smaller animals and children.

In addition to the illustrious Leo, some of Crockett's other famous dogs included his all-time favorite dog, Crockett's Red, and another personal favorite, Rusty. Lummox, Greyboy, Crockett's Sue, Rascal, Hammer and Boss were still other favorites on the Crockett roster. Boss lived to be eleven years old and went out fighting when he was killed by a boar. Other great Crockett-Plotts include the buckskin-colored Crockett's Buck, and his mother Crockett's June, along with Cullowhee Gal. As with the other members of the Big Five, the list of all-time great Crockett-Plott hounds is too lengthy to include them all.

Crockett spent the rest of his life with his wife and family raising and hunting these magnificent canines near their home in Franklin, North Carolina. Like his fellow Big Five members, Crockett was a very intelligent and talented man. He had the talent to pursue almost any career he desired but preferred instead to work outdoors. He spent most of his career, when he was not hunting, working as a logger, farmer and nightwatchman.

Taylor was a tremendous advocate of boar hunting, and he played an integral role in gaining official recognition of the wild hog as a big game animal. He and his dogs killed several of the biggest hogs ever seen in the southern mountains, including one that weighed over four hundred pounds. He kept the head of this huge boar mounted in his home.

In his later years Taylor Crockett devoted a great deal of his time to preserving and protecting his beloved Nantahala Mountains from mining and timber companies. The Nantahala range is the southernmost link of the Appalachian chain, sitting squarely on the North Carolina–Georgia border. Over 200,000 acres of the Nantahala Mountains are National Forest Service–owned land, and Crockett had the foresight to make sure they were preserved and protected for the use of the general public.

In 1978 Crockett told the *Atlanta Journal* his reasons for protecting this splendid region: "I think it's the aesthetic reasons that are most important for keeping this land in wilderness. I have friends who are psychologically beaten by living in the city, and they can come here for a few days and get well again."

Like his friend Gola Ferguson, who he often hunted with, Taylor Crockett was a true renaissance man—an intelligent, multitalented, athletic, tough and articulate man who was

Taylor Crockett's Rusty.

always willing to help others. John Jackson, who first met Crockett in 1980 and remained close to him until his death, describes Taylor as "the most remarkable man I have ever met and I want to honor him by perpetuating the legacy of his wonderful dogs."

That pretty much says it all, doesn't it? What better way is there to honor a friend?

Taylor Crockett remained remarkably active his entire life. John Jackson recalled that at the age of seventy-six Crockett jogged almost an entire day while following his dogs on a hunt in the rugged Deep Gap and Standing Indian Wilderness area on the North Carolina–Georgia border. Taylor Crockett had a stroke while mowing his yard in 1996, and he died shortly afterward at the age of eighty-eight. His was a life well lived—a life full of adventure, friends, family and fine old-time Plott hounds. His dogs, the Crockett-Plotts, remain today some of the best living examples of the old-time Plott dog.

Greyboy, another Taylor Crockett favorite, and a fine example of the old-time Plott dog.

Taylor Crockett with Rascal.

Smoky Mountain Sue, a superb Crockett-Plott equally skilled at hunting boar or bear.

ISAIAH KIDD

The fifth member of the Big Five is Isaiah Kidd. He was the only member of this elite group who did not call the state of North Carolina home. Isaiah Kidd was born December 11, 1882, in Beckley, West Virgina, a remote mountainous region brimming with wild game. Early on, he acquired the love of the hunt and obtained hunting dogs from some timber cutters working near his home. Ironically, these laborers hailed from the mountains of North Carolina. The dogs they gave him were brindle dogs, almost certainly of Plott descent. At the time, Kidd was unaware of the Plott hound breed, but he was nevertheless impressed with these dogs. He used them and others to hunt with for several years.

Isaiah was an accomplished carpenter and building contractor by trade, but he was elected sheriff of Raleigh County, West Virgina, in 1925. He held this office until 1929. Like fellow Big Five member Gola Ferguson, Kidd was a multitalented and good-humored fellow. Being a sheriff was a stressful job, and in 1927 Kidd's wife encouraged him to take some time off to relax a bit.

Kidd had heard that there was some excellent bear and boar hunting in the North Carolina mountains and decided to go there to see for himself. He traveled to the Slick Rock Wilderness area in far Western North Carolina, near the Tennessee border, to test his skills. It was here that Kidd met a game warden by the name of Cody Plott, who told him the story of the Plott bear hounds and allowed him to witness firsthand how his Plott dogs performed on the hunt. Kidd got a bad case of "Plott hound fever" and was not going home without some Plott dogs of his own. He brought two of them

A Taylor Crockett–Plott, name unknown.

back with him. Later Cody Plott introduced Kidd to both Von, George and John Plott, and he struck up an immediate friendship with the brothers.

Kidd obtained dogs from Von Plott, and perhaps from John Plott too. Kidd told Plott historian Frank Methven that he also bought a Plott hound from L.M. Patton of Iowa, who had originally gotten his stock from Von Plott as well. Eventually Kidd came back to North Carolina and visited with Gola Ferguson and other notable old-time hunters. It is believed that Kidd received Plott hounds from Ferguson too. Using those illustrious bloodlines as his foundation stock, Kidd devoted his energies toward developing his own outstanding Plott hounds on his West Virginia farm. Kidd threw himself full-throttle into learning everything he could about the science of dog breeding. He used a book titled *The New Art of Breeding Better Dogs* by Phillip and Kyle Onstott as his road map to mastering this art. Kidd was very scientific and analytical in his approach, and with the help of his wife, he kept detailed records of his work.

Over the next forty or so years Kidd would become the finest dog breeder of his era. As Plott dog expert John Jackson told me,

> *Genetics do not lie. To be a master dog breeder is a special talent. One that few people have the time or talent to master. The best way not to lose your best traits is to avoid out-crossing. It takes thirty years to fully develop your own strain. John Plott did. Gola Ferguson did. Taylor Crockett did. So did Isaiah Kidd—probably none better than Isaiah Kidd. He was a uniquely talented man who was far ahead of his time.*

Isaiah Kidd with one of his Plott pups.

Kidd was so skilled that even though he had received quite a bit of Von Plott stock over the years, he became even better than Von in somehow keeping the obvious "houndy" traits from being visible in his bloodlines. Jackson wrote in *Full Cry* that Kidd "was at least fifty years ahead of others in terms of his knowledge of genetics and his scientific breeding practices."

Kidd also firmly believed that there was simply no way that the early Plott family, with only five original dogs, could have kept their lineage totally pure with no outside infusions for over two hundred years. Kidd made a speech on this topic at one of the early National Plott Hound Association breed day events. He also wrote eloquently and succinctly in a 1960 letter to Frank Methven regarding his overall thoughts on

Plott hounds: "I have a pack of Plott hounds that I hunt on bear, cat and coon. If I knew of any better dogs I would have them."

When Isaiah retired from his contracting business, he and his wife bought a farm in a beautiful valley near Sinks Grove, West Virgina, with a stunning view of the massive Peters Mountain range. They spent the rest of their lives there raising their family and their uniquely brindle dogs. Various shades of brindle are common to the Plott breed, with the dark brindle being most common. But Kidd's dogs were known for their gray, light brindle coats, almost zebra-like in appearance. He once bred a dog whose base coat was nearly buttermilk in color, with stunning black stripes.

But it was not just appearance that made the Kidd dogs special. Like Crockett and other members of the Big Five, he was much more interested in performance than appearance. Kidd was consumed with the need for his dogs to have superb hunting and fighting skills. And they did. Nothing else was acceptable. Kidd had many national champion and award-winning dogs in his lifetime. His bloodlines and pups were some of the most desired in the United States. Even today Plott dog enthusiasts look for these old-time bloodlines to breed their dogs with. Some of Kidd's best-known dogs include Kidd's Daisy, Kidd's Rock, Jeff, Old Belle, Crying Sam and Brindle Boy, just to name a few. Kidd recalled to Steve Fielder that Old Belle had once stuck with and fought a tough "walking" bear for more than three days—even after the bear had killed five other top members of the Kidd pack, including the legendary Crying Sam.

In his later years, thanks in large part to the late Clyde Neader, Kidd was able to maintain close relationships with the other surviving members of the Big Five—Von Plott, Gola Ferguson and Taylor Crockett. Neader, a devoted Plott dog man and charter member of the APA, appreciated the living history of these great men. He devoted a lot of his personal time to taking them to visit each other. In doing so, he learned a lot himself and developed memories that he would treasure the remainder of his life. It was Isaiah Kidd who somewhat jokingly gave Neader credit for "the socializing of Von Plott." Von Plott referred to Neader as "Needum" because Clyde always needed some information or insight on dogs from Von. I would love to have heard some of those conversations.

By the time of his death in 1967, Isaiah Kidd had more than fulfilled his dream of becoming a master dog breeder. He and his dogs were nationally famous—and rightfully so. Like other Big Five members—Von Plott in 1963, John Plott in 1959, Gola Ferguson in 1960 and Taylor Crockett in 1962—Kidd was the proud 1961 recipient of the prestigous Methven Big Game Award. This was only one of many awards and accomplishments he achieved during his amazing lifetime. Like his unique dogs, Isaiah Kidd was one of a kind, and he is a proud and worthy addition to the elite Big Five of Plott hound history.

The prestigous members of the Big Five share many common characteristics. In addition to their monumental contributions to the legacy of the Plott hound, they were each uniquely talented individuals with strong, charismatic and colorful personalities. They unfortunately also share another characteristic in that virtually none of their direct family members chose to perpetuate their family Plott dog legacy to any appreciable extent.

Kidd's Crying Sam, one of four great Kidd-Plott hounds all killed on the same bear hunt.

However, we are extremely fortunate and grateful that the Big Five proudly advanced the Plott hound into the golden age of Plott dog history. More importantly, we are fortunate that there were many other individuals outside of those celebrated families who were willing and able to carry the Plott hound legacy deep into the twentieth century and beyond.

Chapter Nine

THE GOLDEN AGE

By the end of World War II, the reputation of the Plott hound was becoming fairly well established in big game hunting circles nationwide. The Plott brothers, especially Von, had dog packs that most agree were among their best ever. The demand for the Plott dog was strong, and Von advertised his hounds for sale in nationwide magazine ads. Sales were apparently brisk, and Von Plott–bred Plott hounds were shipped by train to customers all over the United States. Gola Ferguson's Plott dogs had also gained widespread fame, thanks in large part to his acclaimed hounds Boss and Tige. Isaiah Kidd's canines, too, were receiving well-deserved recognition. And Taylor Crockett, home from the war, was well on his way to establishing his legendary old-time Plott hound line.

Newspaper and magazine articles in the *New York Times*, *Field and Stream*, *Outdoor Life* and *Sports Afield*, among others, all extolled the virtues of the Plott hound and their hunting exploits. Jim Gasque devoted several chapters in his 1947 book *Hunting and Fishing in the Great Smokies* to big game hunting in the North Carolina mountains, and he devoted an entire chapter specifically to the Plott hound and Plott family.

Yet, even with all these well-deserved nationwide accolades and dog sales, the Plott hound was not yet an officially recognized dog breed. This was soon to change. The era starting in the early to mid-1940s and extending through the late 1960s is considered by many to be "the golden age" of the Plott bear hound, and for good reason, as the breed finally gained official and national recognition during this period.

Hack Smithdeal's purchase of Plott hounds from John and Little George Plott, and subsequent purchases from Von Plott, resulted in Smithdeal having one of the largest and most prestigious packs of Plott hounds in the United States by 1946. In fact, some experts feel that this may have been the best pack of Plott hounds ever to exist. That is debatable, but there is no doubt that this was a powerhouse pack of Plott hounds and probably the largest and best of the 1940s.

Smithdeal was an avid bear hunter. But unlike a lot of other equally skilled or superior hunters, Hack had the money to hunt all over the country, as well as the means to purchase any bear dogs that caught his fancy. Many credit Smithdeal with being a

Smithdeal's Cricket, a notable Smithdeal-Plott later sold to Dale Brandenburger.

premier dog breeder. I don't believe that to be the case. Instead, I believe that he simply knew what he wanted and had the financial means to obtain it. He also had the money to own and maintain superb kennel facilities and to employ the top hunting guides, dog handlers and breeders to assist him in his quest for the perfect hunt and the perfect dog.

That is not to say that Smithdeal did not have superb Plott dogs. He did. Nor can it be said that no champion hounds were bred out of his kennels—there were several. Some of his more celebrated dogs include Smithdeal's Nigger, Old Heavy, Smithdeal's Drum and Smithdeal's Cricket, to name just a few. And there were many more.

But unlike the master breeders in the Big Five, Smithdeal had little time or ability to develop and refine his own stock. He chose instead to start at the top buying only the best, and he proceeded forward from there. There is nothing wrong with that. Many others would have done the same thing had they had the money to do so. This by no means is a slight on Smithdeal, who I think played a key role in the Plott hound gaining national recognition and in ushering in the dawn of the golden age of the Plott breed. But it was his ability to hunt all over the United States using only the best Plott dogs and guides—not his breeding skills—that played a huge part in the breed gaining not only national fame, but also official recognition from the United Kennel Club.

It should also be noted that the registering of some Plott dogs, such as Smithdeal's Nigger, with a racial slur is a regrettable part of Plott hound history. But in fairness, this was more of a reflection of the time and place than a case of individual racism. In fact, the Smithdeal dog was supposedly named by one of Smithdeal's black employees, who when seeing the pup for the first time exclaimed, "That puppy looks just like a little nigger baby!" Nevertheless, that does not make this type of thing right. No official breed registry today would register a dog under an offensive name. Nor do I know any Plott hound enthusiast today—and we are of all races and genders—who would encourage or condone this type of thinking.

In 1946 the Michigan Wildlife Department was considering officially opening bear hunting season in its state. As a test run, the department invited Hack Smithdeal and Von Plott to bring their Plott hounds to lead the initial hunt. Supposedly the legendary Plott hound, Smithdeal's Nigger, a littermate to John Plott's Mack, was one of the many star hounds who excelled on this hunt. The hunt proved to be a resounding success and Michigan officially opened its bear hunting season the following year.

Many Midwestern hunters and dog breeders became almost obsessed with obtaining Plott hounds of their own. Three notable Midwestern Plott hound men were instrumental in the Plott hound gaining official recognition from the United Kennel Club in 1946. Alva Stegenga of Iona, Michigan, first contacted the UKC in 1945 about registering the breed. He was later joined by L.M. Patton of Iowa and Leonard Moffet of Illinois in spearheading the effort for official breed recognition. (All these men had purchased their first Plott hounds from Von Plott magazine ads.) Back in North Carolina, Gola Ferguson and others also pushed the UKC to register the Plott hound.

Their efforts were rewarded on February 12, 1946, when the UKC officially opened its stud files for Plott hound registration. This was no small feat, and these men and others deserve a great deal of thanks and praise for this achievement.

The first official standards for the Plott hound were as follows:

OFFICIAL UNITED KENNEL CLUB PLOTT HOUND STANDARD

This standard was framed for the purpose of furnishing suggestions for breeding to the breeders, in their aims toward improving the breed, to higher ideals in their breeding. To try and establish a nationwide breed of this particular hound strain of bloodlines to look alike and to have a universal conformation.

HEAD–Carried well up, dome moderately flat, moderate width between and above eyes. Ears set moderately high and of medium length, soft and no erectile power. Eyes brown or hazel, prominent, no drooping eyelids. Muzzle moderate length but not square.
SHOULDERS–Muscular and sloping to indicate speed and strength.

Hack Smithdeal on left and Von Plott on right, while on their first Michigan bear hunt in 1946.

CHEST–Deep with adequate lung space.

BACK–Slightly arched, well muscled and strong, not roached.

HIPS–Smooth, round, proportionately wide, flanks gracefully arched, muscular quarters and loins.

TAIL–Moderately heavy, strong at root, tapering there, rather long without brush, carried free, well up, saber like.

FRONT LEGS–Straight, smooth, forearm muscular. Straight at knees, perfectly in line with upper leg.

HIND LEGS–Strong and muscular above hock, slightly bent at hock, no cowhock, speedy shaped and graceful.

FEET–Round solid, cat foot, well padded and knucked, set directly under leg.

COLOR AND COAT–Smooth haired, fine, glossy, but thick enough for protection in cold wind and water. Brindle or brindle with black saddle. Some white on chest or feet permissable.

VOICE–Open trailing, bawl and chop.

HEIGHT–Males: 22 to 25 inches at shoulder. Females: 21 to 24 inches at shoulder.

WEIGHT–Males: 50 to 65 pounds. Females: 40 to 55 pounds.

CHARACTERISTICS OF THIS BREED–Active, fast, bright, confident, courageous, vicious fighters on game, super treeing instinct, take readily to water, alert, quick to learn, have a great endurance and beauty.

The United Kennel Club, Inc., wishes to thank all the breeders and fanciers for their splendid cooperation and the great interest in this breed that was shown by all and the efforts that they made which made it possible to officially recognize this fine breed, the Plott hound.

POINTS

HEAD	15	ELBOWS	5
NECK	5	LEGS & FEET	15
SHOULDERS	10	COAT & COLOR	5
CHEST & RIBS	10	TAIL	5
BACK & LOINS	15	GENERAL MAKE-UP	5
HIND QUARTERS	10	TOTAL	100

Reprinted with permission of the United Kennel Club.

It should be noted that developing official or even unofficial breed standards and recognition are complex issues and somewhat difficult to understand or explain. But as I understand it, a national club such as the UKC or American Kennel Club gives permission to individuals (like Patton and Moffet) or to a specific breed organization like the National Plott Hound Association to write or create a standard for their respective breed. The national club then grants the individuals or breed organization unofficial conditional recognition of the breed. After proving their worth by longevity

Some of the first Plott hounds ever registered (left to right): Owens's King Plott, Plott's Dan and Bess. In back is Balsam Kate, pup of Dan and Bess.

and submitting reams of paperwork—which can take months, or even years—the breed organization is given official status as the parent club or club of choice in representing the breed. The parent club or club of choice is then officially recognized as the breed representative.

So in the case of the Plott hound, thanks to the initial efforts of the above mentioned individuals, the Plott dog was first allowed conditional recognition as founding stock in 1946. This opened up the UKC rolls for official conditional registration. Buckskin-colored dogs were allowed in the intitial conditional breed standard. That would unfortunately soon change.

L.M. Patton had the honor of having the first UKC-registered Plott hound, a gyp named Bess. Bess was whelped from Hazelwood Kate II and Hazelwood Heavy, who were Von Plott–bred dogs. Other charter owners of the first single registered purebred Plotts included H. Von Plott, John D. Plott, Sam Plott, Gola P. Ferguson, H.T. Crockett, Hack Smithdeal, Isaiah Kidd, Regan Wells, John Owens, Leonard Moffett, Rickey Red Eagle and A.F. Stegenga.

A.F. Stegenga was further rewarded for his efforts in getting the Plott hound UKC certified when his prize Plott hound Lucky Strike was featured on the cover of the March 1946 edition of the *UKC Bloodlines Magazine*. The Plott hound had now officially hit the big time, the real major leagues of the dog world. The fame and popularity of the breed would further skyrocket over the next few decades.

In September of 1946, another Midwesterner, Dale Brandenburger of Illinois, bought his first Plott hound from Alva Stegenga. Shortly afterward he purchased several dogs with Von Plott bloodlines. This would be the start of a literal Plott hound factory—Pioneer Kennels—which would make Brandenburger famous.

About 1949, Brandenburger traveled to Plott Valley to meet the Plott brothers and learn more about their dogs. He also visited with Gola Ferguson and other local Plott hound breeders. Brandenburger then traveled "over the mountain" to Johnson City, Tennessee, to visit with Hack Smithdeal. It was here that Brandenburger first saw Smithdeal's large Plott hound pack and his most famous dog—Smithdeal's Nigger. Brandenburger somehow convinced Smithdeal to sell Nigger to him, and he borrowed

A.F. Stegenga's Lucky Strike, the first Plott hound pictured on the cover of *UKC Bloodlines Magazine* in March 1946.

money from his sister to pay for the dog. This would be the first of several transactions between the two men that would further solidify both of their places in Plott hound history. Dale would next buy Smithdeal's top female dog, Cricket, who was well known as a fierce bear fighter. He then purchased the last son of Smithdeal's Old Heavy—a Plott hound he renamed Timber—from either Jake Hampton or Henry Haldeman.

These purchases would form the foundation for the Pioneer Kennels' celebrated Plott hound franchise. For the next forty-plus years the kennel would sell literally thousands of Plott hounds, as well as numerous award-winning championship dogs. Along with the above mentioned dogs, some of the more famous hounds to come out of or be affiliated with Pioneer Kennels include Big Lucky (who was the first Plott hound to be a coon dog night champion) and Pioneer Jake. Also worthy of mention are Brandenburger's Chief, along with Sashay Moon I and II, Brindle Major and probably the most famous of them all, Pioneer Drum. Pioneer Drum, like most of Brandenburger's Von Plott–bred stock, was distinctly hound-like in appearance with very long ears and loose skin. But unlike some of Brandenburger's other hounds, Drum was huge, almost twice the size of a normal Plott hound.

The UKC magazine *Coonhound Bloodlines* publishes a yearly special issue devoted entirely to Plott hounds. Every few years they rank the top ten Plott stud dogs of all time.

Smithdeal's Old Heavy. Note the large size and "houndy" appearance of this dog.

Pioneer Drum almost always heads the list, including their most recent one, which was compiled in July 2000. Drum was born in 1957 and in his lifetime sired 1,035 pups and produced 19 Night Champion Coon dogs, twenty-five show champions and one Grand Show champion, as well as two water champions. In addition to Drum, Brandenburger had two other Plott hounds on the top ten list, Pioneer Mike, born in 1960, and Pioneer Slim, born in 1967. These two studs between them sired 1,563 pups and produced 70 champion or grand champion dogs.

Dale Brandenburger stated in 1983 that he had sold more Plott hounds from his kennels than any other breeder in Plott hound history. Few can dispute that claim. Many Plott hounds spread across the nation today can trace their bloodlines back to Pioneer Kennels. Dale Brandenburger undoubdtedly played a significant role in the Plott hound gaining nationwide recognition.

The National Plott Hound Association, or NPHA, was formed in September 1954 in Leafy Oaks, Ohio. Dale Brandenburger and another well-known Plott hound man, Joe Storts, were instrumental in the founding of the club. H.L. Brown was the first president of the group, and the purposes of the NPHA were clearly and simply stated in the initial bylaws of their constitution:

> —*To influence the breeding of better and finer PLOTT HOUNDS.*
> —*To create a better knowledge of what a good PLOTT HOUND really is.*
> —*To influence the raising of better PLOTT HOUNDS.*

Dale Brandenburger with Big Lucky, the first nighttime Plott coon dog champion.

Carl Brandenburger on left and Dale Brandenburger on right, with their famous Plott hounds, Pioneer Drum, Ozark Chief, Pioneer Tiger and Cherokee Joe. Note the size of Drum compared to the other hounds.

—To create better trade practices among and between the breeders of PLOTT HOUNDS.
—To educate the public to the fact that the Registered PLOTT HOUND is by far the best and more desirable coonhound to own.

The NPHA was officially recognized by the UKC as the club of choice for the Plott hound. This meant that the NPHA breed standard would become the officially recognized unconditional standard for the Plott hound breed and would further legitimize the dog. This was yet another golden age milestone for the breed. The organization grew rapidly, and with bear hunting seasons open nearby in both Michigan and eventually Wisconsin, they quickly began to expand their interests to include big game hunting—not just coon hunting—for their club. The group soon had nationwide membership and began an annual gathering known as Plott Days that was usually held in August. It provided Plott hound owners from across the nation the opportunity to meet and "talk Plotts." Just as importantly, the NPHA provided various types of coon hunting competitions to crown annual champion Plott hounds. These events proved to be extremely popular.

In 1959 they published their first annual "yearbook" that told hunting and historical stories of the breed. The publication also listed award-winning Plott hounds and owners in various competitive classes. Also included in the yearbook were ads for top kennels and breeders that provided even more opportunity for the general public to purchase and have easier access to the Plott hound. One of the most prestigious and anxiously anticipated later features of the yearbook, and indeed the organization as a whole, was the Frank Methven Big Game Award. This award is given annually to the individual who is considered the best hunter and/or who has contributed the most to the sport of big game hunting with Plott hounds. It is a highly coveted award whose list of winners reads like a Plott hound historical hall of fame. All of the Big Five members made the list, as well as most of the early Plott family, including Johannes, Henry, John and Montraville Plott. Of course, Hack Smithdeal and Dale Brandenburger are included, as are many other more contemporary Plott hound legends who we will discuss shortly. A complete list of Methven winners is included in the appendix, as well as on the NPHA website and in the NPHA and American Plott Association annual yearbooks

Controversy with the NPHA first reared its ugly head in 1958, when the group asked the UKC to remove the buckskin-colored Plott hound from breed standards. Buckskin was an acceptable color in the original 1946 standard—and rightfully so. But some within the organization were concerned that breeders, in an effort to produce more buckskin-colored Plott hounds, had added redbone hound infusions in the Plott hound lineage. If true, this was simply unacceptable.

It was a complex problem that came down to two simple questions:

1. Should a traditional Plott hound color that dated back to 1750 be eliminated just to correct the alleged redbone infusion issue?

2. How could the NPHA keep the buckskin color in the breed standard, yet somehow police the breeders who were supposedly illegally weakening the breed?

The NPHA felt that there was no way to police all of the breeders so they convinced the UKC to remove the buckskin color from their breed standard in 1958. Many Plott hound experts agree that the removal of the buckskin Plott was a dark day in breed history. Others will say that it needed to be done to preserve the lineage. I tend to side with the buckskin faction myself. I think it is a valid color and a true part of Plott hound history. More importantly, both Isaiah Kidd and Von Plott were advocates of the buckskin Plott hound. If they felt that way—and there is documentation to prove that they did—then how can anyone else question it?

Two other major kennel clubs, the AKC and PKC, eventually recognized the buckskin in their breed standards, but the UKC continues to refuse to do so. While indeed a serious issue, it fortunately did not adversely affect the growing interest in the Plott hound.

Another key to the growth and popularity of the Plott hound during the golden age era was the start of nighttime raccoon hunts, or field trial competitions. These contests, also known as "nite hunts" or wild coon hunts, further expanded the role of the Plott hound to include the small game hunting arena, primarily featuring raccoons. Again, it was Dale Brandenburger, along with Elwood Overbeck and Kentuckian Colonel Bennie Moore, among others, who was instrumental in launching these events. (See the Glossary for a definition of these competitions.)

These events provided an option for anyone, anywhere, owning a Plott hound to test their dogs on trailing, treeing and baying an animal, as raccoons were common nationwide. It also provided an opportunity for owners to test their hounds with little chance for serious injury or death to the dog. These contests soon became wildly popular nationwide and still are today. Elwood Overbeck's Lucky and Brandenburger's Big Lucky were the first two Plott hounds to to win night champion coon hunting events.

The list of other Midwesterners who played key roles in Plott hound history is a long one. There is no way to include them all here. But several individuals must be mentioned. Let's start with Jim and Jerry Pfister of Great Bend, Kansas. The Pfister brothers raised top-notch Plott hounds, especially coon dogs. Since there were few bears in the Midwest, except in Michigan and Wisconsin, most Plott enthusiasts in this area focused their interests on coon hunting. The Pfister Plotts were second to none in this arena. But they were also avid big game hunters, often traveling to the far west to hunt with government hunter and guide Willis Butolph. Their hounds soon became skilled big game dogs, too. The Pfisters got most of their original Plott stock from John Owens.

Owens, of Bloomfield, Iowa, was one of the earliest Midwestern Plott hound breeders, and he developed a reputation as one of the best in the region. He favored the colder-nosed strain of Plott hound that originated from Von Plott stock and he would accept no other dogs in his kennel. He, too, was renowned for his superb coon dogs.

Another famed heartland Plott dog man from the golden age era was Clyde Bounds of Freeport, Illinois. Clyde was known not only for his outstanding Plott hounds but also for pioneering the use of electronic dog tracking collars. This innovation alone is worthy of his recognition in Plott hound history. It has literally saved the lives of many dogs that otherwise would have been lost or stolen. (We will discuss these collars and other hunting methods in Chapter Eleven.)

But Bounds's Plott hounds were equally impressive. His Black River Bolly ranks as one of the finest Plott dogs of all time. Bolly was often referred to in the Great Lakes

Clyde Bounds with Black River Bolly, Ruby and Clyde. Bolly was one of the most famous Plott hounds in the Midwest.

Leroy Haug, who developed the Swampland strain of Plotts, seen here with Swampland Star.

region as "the Golden Boy of Bear Dogs." Clyde said in the 2003 *APA Brindle Book* that "Bolly was born to hunt bear." An early registered Plott hound, Bolly was a light golden-brindled Plott dog that stood about twenty-seven inches tall and weighed around seventy-five pounds. Bounds also noted that the best female Plott hound he ever owned was a gyp named Ruby. Other exceptional Bounds-Plott hounds included Easy and Duke. Clyde Bounds is at or near the top of any golden age Midwestern Plott hound breeding and hunting list.

Other noteworthy Midwestern Plott pioneers were Leroy Haug, Roy Sing, Joe Lukas, Ernst Polly and Dwayne and Steve Herd. Still others worthy of mention include Henry Haldeman, Ross Snoake and Robert Daughtery. But no list of esteemed Midwestern Plott hound men would be complete without Everette Weems of Salem, Illinois. Weems has long been recognized as not only a superb dog breeder and hunter, but also as a fine and honorable gentleman. Many Plott dog experts feel that Everette's dog, Weems's Plott John, is the genetic blueprint that all Plott hounds should be bred for. Others may debate that point, but no one can argue that Everette Weems produced some of the best contemporary Plott hounds the Plott world has ever seen. Weems's stock originated from Von Plott, Gola Ferguson and Dale Brandenburger. It would ultimately produce such remarkable Plott hounds as Plott's Suzi, the red-brindled Weems's John, Plott's Punie and probably his two most famous dogs—Butch and Jill. Weems has several NPHA Hall of Fame dogs and has won many awards himself for a lifetime of contributions to the Plott hound. These

Everette Weems with Weems's John, a dog considered by many to be the perfect genetic blueprint for all Plott hounds.

Midwestern golden age Plott men and others are largely responsible for the Plott hound as we know it today.

The tidal wave of Plott hound popularity next surged toward the West Coast and Rocky Mountain states. By the early 1950s Plott hounds were being commonly used in the West by professional contract hunters to hunt a variety of big game, including bears, mountain lions, wolves, bobcats and coyotes. Bears were a two-fold problem in the West for both farmers and businessmen. Farmers were plagued by the loss of their livestock to big game. The lumber barons had issues with bears ripping bark from their trees, reducing profits and scaring work crews. This resulted in the government, as well as the big corporations, contracting hunters to eliminate the problems. It quickly proved to be a rather lucrative business for expert hunters and their Plott dogs. Furthermore, as the reputations of both the hunters and their Plott dogs grew, they were able to pick up additional business as hunting guides for clients around the country.

Probably the earliest contract hunter to use Plott hounds on the West Coast was North Carolina native Homer Wright. Wright had first worked on Von Plott's farm in the late 1930s, but by the early 1940s he had moved to Washington state to find more work. Von Plott sent Wright some Plott pups in about 1943, and by 1946 Homer had a fine pack of Plott hounds. Wright and his son Hank were two of the first to use Plott hounds for cougar hunting in the Pilchuck River and Snohomish River basins. But they were *the* first individuals to bring Plott hounds to Washington state.

Other famed West Coast Plott men with North Carolina ties were Ray Jones, who was kin to the Reece family of lep dog fame, and Bud Hyatt, who was closely related to

North Carolina native Homer Wright, who later moved to Washington state in the mid-1940s and brought the first Plott hounds there. Wright was a renowned West Coast contract hunter.

the Plott family. Jones and Hyatt were known for their fine Plott hounds, and Hyatt was especially devoted to protecting the integrity of the breed.

Ed "Purehate" Watkins was another rugged Western hunter and Plott man. He earned his nickname when a friend described him as being "six foot and three inches of muscle and brawn and 190 pounds of pure hate." Perhaps this came in part because he once killed a full-grown, angry, but otherwise healthy bear while armed only with a knife. Watkins was clearly not a man who would easily walk away from a fight. Two of his favorite Plott dogs, Old Smoke and Bucko, were both eventually killed by bears.

The six-foot, four-inch Gene Young and his Plott dog Lead, along with Ray Fain and his Plott hound Little Judy, were also well known in the region. Little Judy was an oddly colored Plott hound, red with a black saddle, but she proved to be a formidable bear dog. She was the runt in a litter of Plott pups from the highly celebrated Demoss-Cascade Plotts and turned out to be perhaps Fain's all-time best bear dog.

Jerry Tuller was one of the most respected guides and Plott men in the Pacific Northwest. His hunting career was unfortunately cut short due to blindness. One of Tuller's dogs, Lil Coke, was called a "near perfect bear dog" by Frank Methven. Tuller once worked with yet another legendary but controversial figure in Plott hound history, Doyle "Dee" Demoss. Demoss was probably the best-known hunting guide, contract hunter, Plott breeder and promoter on the West Coast. The Demoss-Plott dogs were of Von Plott lineage and formed the foundation stock for what would come to be known as "the Cascade Plott line." One of the more famous dogs to come from this line was named Cascade Big Timber. Big Timber was later sold by Demoss to Knoxville, Tennesse attorney Oliver Smith, who also owned a lot of Smithdeal-Plott hound stock. Smith combined the Cascade stock with his already well-established pack, and the result was some of the most exceptional Plott hounds on the East Coast.

The Cascade-Plotts and their owner Dee Demoss would achieve further national acclaim in the 1960s when they appeared on the ABC network television show *The American Sportsman*. This popular program was hosted by Curt Gowdy and was shown weekly across the United States on Saturday afternoons. The show featured top hunting and fishing guides with their celebrity guests, who were filmed hunting or fishing around the world. In this particular episode, Demoss and his Cascade-Plotts—led by his favorite strike dog Cascade Sparkle—took Oakland Raider quarterback Daryl Lamonica on a successful West Coast bear and big cat hunt.

Demoss and his dogs would gain worldwide acclaim in the late 1960s when they were recruited to kill some man-eating bears in Japan. It seems that numerous grizzly sized bears, most weighing over 1,200 pounds, had killed an average of sixty Japanese villagers annually for several years. The Japanese government had exhaused its efforts to correct this tragic problem until it learned of Demoss and his Plott pack. The government hired Demoss and his dogs to resolve the situation—and they did, in short order. Demoss, accompanied by Jerry Tuller and their ten Plott dogs, quickly killed ten of these monsters and they became idols of the Japanese villagers. Von Plott had often wondered how his Plott dogs would fare against the Western grizzly or a bear of similar size. Demoss, Tuller and their Plott hounds proved that they would do just fine.

Upon his return to America, Demoss and his Plott line would become even more famous, as his reputation as a top breeder and hunting guide continued to grow. Unfortunately there would later be controversy over the original lineage of his dogs and some have questioned the legitimacy of their bloodlines. I won't comment on that argument either way except to say this. Only those that were actually there know the real truth. Dog experts, lawyers and kennel clubs can sort the rest of it out. But regardless of their origins, legitimate or otherwise, the Cascade-Plotts were, and are, some fine dogs and Doyle Demoss deserves at least some credit for that. Plus, right or wrong, he deserves a prominent place in West Coast Plott dog history simply for the worldwide recognition that he helped bring to the breed.

Someone that *was* there and someone who hunted and worked with all of these West Coast Plott legends is hunting guide, writer and Plott hound proponent Frank Methven. Methven's family was originally from Kentucky, but they moved to California when Frank was a child. The Methvens are one of the few families today that can say they hunted with both Montraville and Von Plott and their old-time Plott hounds. Frank's father, a noted contract hunter and guide, his grandfather, great-grandfather and uncle all hunted with what they called "brindle mountain curs" and kept a hunting lodge not far from the Plott family homeplace in the North Carolina mountains.

It was here that the Methvens were initially exposed to Plott hounds when they first hunted with Montraville and Von Plott in about 1908. When he was eighty years old, Frank Methven's Uncle John recalled this hunt in a letter to Frank, saying in part:

> *I was twelve years old at the time. The family that lived near there* [the Methven cabin] *and used to raise these dogs was named Plott, and they raised what was called the Plott dogs. There was a boy on the hunt that was my age. I believe his name was Vaughn. We did not go with the dogs and the men on horseback. We waited at the camp to see the bear brought back on a horse. I believe the name of the father of this other boy was Mont. I recall that he had a beautiful horse. He was very proud of his horse. We did not take any of our dogs as we had a long train ride and a long wagon ride to get back to the hunting cabin.*

With roots like these, it is easy to understand how the Methven family name later became synonymous with Plott hounds. After serving in World War II, Frank Methven bought his first Plott hound, an unregistered dog, in California in the late 1940s or early 1950s. His fascination with the breed would only grow stronger from there. Shortly after that Frank heard of the great bear hunting in Washington state and moved his family there. It was there that Methven would carry on his family's tradition as expert contract hunters and guides. He would later obtain still more Plott hounds from both Von Plott and others. Methven was well known for always having top Plott dogs, including his favorite, Battle Cry, who we will discuss in Chapter Eleven. Methven is an accomplished writer; he is the author of two books and has been a columnist for *American Cooner* for over forty years. In 1955 he established the Frank Methven Big Game Award, given annually by the NPHA to honor his father, grandfathers and uncle.

But for all his amazing achievements—and there are many—Frank Methven will always be best remembered as an eloquent and articulate spokesman, advocate and historian for the Plott hound breed. Few, if any, individuals possess his knowledge of West Coast Plott hound history. And, like the gentleman that he is, he gladly shares his knowledge of the breed and hunting with anyone who asks.

Still more Western hunters would learn of the lore of the Plott hound from Methven and others like him, while others would learn of the dog from magazine stories and ads or from other Eastern and Midwestern hunters who came West to hunt. With the Western and Midwestern puppy factories producing Plott hounds in record numbers, as well as those available from the East Coast originators of the breed, there were plenty of fine Plott dogs available for purchase. By the 1960s, such eminent professional contract

Luis Fred Albiser, a West Coast government hunter from 1960 to 1995, with his Plott hounds Boney and Tonka, along with three bears taken on a hunt.

hunters as Luis Fred Absher, Frank Staab, Doc Kimet, Olen Greer and Willis Butolph all used Plott hounds in their work. The Plott dogs had found yet another new home in the far west.

Meanwhile, back in the Southeast, thanks to the continued efforts of the Big Five, the Plott hound network now extended from New England to Florida. By 1963, the Big Five had lost two of their esteemed members in John Plott, who died in 1959, and Gola Ferguson, who passed away in 1962. But thanks to their many friends and protégés their legacy continues even today.

For example, John Bowen obtained his first Plott hound, a dog named Rube, from the Plott family in 1946. He returned with Rube to his Virgina farm and embarked on a long career in the dog business. Von Plott once supposedly said that Rube was the best bear hound he had ever seen. A granddaughter of Rube, a female that Bowen called Dolly, was one of his top bear dogs. Other well-respected Bowen-Plotts included Twinkle Toes and Bowen's Jack. John Bowen's Plott hounds were in on more than sixty bear kills in the swamplands of eastern North Carolina.

Three Eastern pioneers of Plott hound history from the last half of the twentieth century—Homan Fielder, Robert Jones and Sam George—obtained their first Plott hounds at about the same time in the mid-1950s. Fielder, a Tennessee native and World War II veteran, moved to Beckley, West Virginia, in about 1946. It was here, in the autumn of 1954, that his lifelong love affair with the Plott dog breed began. A friend of Fielder's, Opal Bennett, had two Plott females—Daisy and June—who would leave a lasting impression on Homan. While hunting in the midst of an early snowstorm with Bennett's two Plott dogs, as well as Homan's own black-and-tan hound, the dogs struck a bear trail. Fielder's dog refused to pursue it, but the Plotts sure did. The two Plott females trailed and fought the bear throughout the night in the worst of blizzard conditions. Only June survived, but Fielder knew right then that he had found his tree dog of choice. He traded a gun to Bennett for June and was in the Plott dog business.

Fielder would later obtain Plott dogs with Von Plott, John Owen and Isaiah Kidd bloodlines. Since Kidd lived nearby, he developed a long lasting friendship with the master breeder. These royal Plott hound bloodlines would form the foundation of an accomplished line of Plott hounds known as the Bear Pen Plotts. Some of Fielder's first dogs were gray-brindled hounds. A couple of his more notable dogs, among others, were Bear Pen Sam and Bear Pen Fancy. Over the next forty years Bear Pen Plotts would be recognized as some of the finest Plott hounds of the era.

Robert Jones, the esteemed hunter and Okeefenokee Swamp guide from Georgia, bought his first Plott hound in 1955, and he named her Dixie Lou. A passion for the Plott dog breed was instilled in him then. For more than half a century, this dedicated Plott man has raised and hunted with some of the best Plott hounds in the South. Robert's dogs have a lot of Von Plott lineage. And like Von, Jones is mostly concerned with what works best for him in a dog. He has proven to be a knowledgeable and articulate spokesman for the Plott breed and for big game hunting. As he quietly but eloquently told me in 2007, "I am very proud of my dogs. Some people may not like them, and that's fine. But I do. And they work well for me. That's really all that matters, isn't it?"

Yes sir, Mr. Jones, I'd say that about sums it up.

West Virginian Sam George got his first Plott hound in 1956. It was a dog named Babe that came from John Plott and Hack Smithdeal stock. This would form the foundation stock for a fine pack of Plott dogs that he would keep for more than fifty years. George lived near Isaiah Kidd and was fortunate to become friends with him. Sam often sat on the Kidds' porch in Sinks Grove, West Virginia, learning about the Plott hound. And who better to learn from? George noted that Mrs. Kidd was very knowledgeable about the Kidd-Plott pack and knew their bloodlines as good or better than her esteemed husband.

From 1956 to today—more than half a century—Sam George has devoted his life to perpetuating the Plott breed. And not just any Plott hound would work for George. He would accept nothing but the best bloodlines, and his stock originated from the best of the best—Von Plott, Isaiah Kidd, John Plott, Gola Ferguson and Taylor Crockett. Very few of even the best Plott hound enthusiasts can claim all of these royal Big Five bloodlines.

George would later become friends with other illustrious names in Plott hound history, men like Robert Jones, Cheyenne Hill, John Jackson and Ellet Bias, to name a few. Other than regular visits to annual Plott events, George has chosen to spend most of his life hunting and raising dogs in West Virginia, and with fine results. As he told me in 2007, "I know the land around there, and I know my dogs. I get my limit [big game] and don't see the need to go anywhere else."

That sure makes sense to me.

Meanwhile, Von Plott, though at an age when most folks are slowing down, remained active in the 1960s, hunting all over the country. His dogs were in demand nationwide. He continued to gain fame in numerous magazine and newspaper articles and his name had become synonomous with the Plott hound breed. Between the dogs he supplied to his own customers and those from Brandenburger's Midwest puppy factory, Von Plott–bred lineage was being produced, sold and registered in record amounts.

One of Von Plott's hunting pals in the 1960s and 1970s was C.E. "Bud" Lyon. Lyon grew up in the mountains of East Tennessee and hunted with hounds from an early age—but never Plotts. However, he can vividly recall the first Plott dogs that he ever saw. In about 1930, Lyon was riding home from school on a school bus when he saw several dogs run down and kill a fox. Lyon was impressed and checked around to find out just what type of hounds they were. He learned intitially that they were known simply as brindle bear dogs. But later, he learned their true name—Plott hounds. These Plotts left a lasting impression on Lyon and he vowed to one day get some of them for himself. Lyon's father was a skilled stonemason who worked briefly for Hack Smithdeal. The next Plott dogs that young Lyon would see were the original Plott dogs that Smithdeal had purchased from John and Little George Plott near the end of World War II. He saw these legendary dogs at a store near his home, and he became even more determined to get some Plotts of his own.

In the late 1950s, after serving in the army and returning home to begin a career in law enforcement, Lyon finally obtained his first Plott hound—one with Gola Ferguson and Von Plott bloodlines—in north Georgia. He then truly recognized the value of the breed and dove headfirst into a life of hunting and breeding Plott hounds. Bud

Plott's Rock, another great Von Plott dog.

drove to Plott Valley in 1958 and struck up a friendship with Von Plott that would last for more than two decades. Lyon received some of Gola Ferguson's last stock in 1962, and two years prior to that he had begun to hunt with Von Plott. Von was in his mid-sixties then, but Bud said that he had never seen anyone love the sound of the hound, or the thrill of the chase, more than Von Plott. Lyon told me in 2007 that "the old man [Von] would get the happiest look on his face when his dogs struck a trail. And he would not stop until the bear was bayed and killed. I have seen him often run all day, without stopping to eat or rest, and even as an old man, he would be the first one to the bear tree." Lyon and Plott participated in several famous Michigan bear

Von Plott and Bud Lyon on one of Von Plott's last bear hunts.

hunts in the early 1960s. Plott's Balsam Rock, one of Von's all-time best stud dogs, was with them on one of these hunts. Lyon was with Von on perhaps his last bear hunt, in eastern North Carolina in the early 1970s.

As their friendship grew, Lyon began to regularly obtain dogs from Von and over the past forty-seven years he has played a key role in the perpetuation of the true Von Plott lineage. Today, Bud Lyon, like his former mentor Von Plott, is an older man himself and remains an active bear hunter and Plott hound breeder. His kennel just produced a seventh-generation litter of genuine Von Plott stock, and he plans to take his pack to Michigan for their annual bear hunt this September. Bud Lyon is also unique in that not only has he become a Plott dog legend himself, but he is also one of the few individuals who can claim to have had friendships and hunted with three of the illustrious Big Five—Von Plott, Taylor Crockett and Isaiah Kidd. He knew the other two members, John Plott and Gola Ferguson, as well. Like so many of the prominent figures in Plott hound history, Bud Lyon has proven to be a gentleman and an eloquent spokesman for the breed, and a man who is totally dedicated to perpetuating the legacy of the Plott hound.

Hack Smithdeal, after being found innocent of a murder charge, was out of the dog business entirely by the early 1960s. Even though his case was clearly one of self-defense, the stress of the trial took its toll on him. As a result, in 1963, he permanently exited the dog business almost as quickly as he had gotten into it, nearly twenty years earlier. But before Smithdeal got out of the dog business, Berlin King, of Ivanhoe, Virginia, bought some Plott hounds from him in 1949. King then developed quite a dog business of his own, selling Plott hounds for the next several decades. His first registered Plott was New River Hammer. His kennels would ultimately rival those of Dale Brandenburger as a top producer of Plott coonhound pups. *UKC Bloodlines Magazine* lists three of King's Plott hounds in their top fifteen all-time best Plott dog stud list.

Taylor Crockett did not care much for dog registration records or awards, nor did he depend on the dog business to make a living. But he too remained a formidable force in the golden age, wreaking havoc on the hog and bear population in the Nantahala range and producing superb Plott hounds and his own legion of supporters. The foremost of these was Lawrence Porterfield from Cleveland, Tennessee. Porterfield early on recognized the value of the old-time Plott hound, and he became fast friends with Crockett. For the rest of his career, Lawrence would keep no other Plott hounds but those from either Taylor Crockett or his Tennessee friend R.C. Roark.

Isaiah Kidd, while in the twilight of his life in the mid-1960s, retained his position as the senior spokesman of the Plott hound world. Like the other Big Five members, he had his own circle of hunters and breeders who swore by his dogs. Fellow West Virginians like Sam George and Homan Fielder would both migrate to the Kidd Farm to learn from the old master.

Others, like the late Clyde Neader, had the foresight to capture this living history before it was lost. Neader, a Missouri native, not only raised fine Plott hounds of his own, like Ozark Cujo, but more importantly spent time recording the legacy of the surviving Big Five and their dogs for future generations. In the 1960s Neader devoted a great deal of his personal time to taking Kidd and Von Plott to visit each other. In the process, he learned a lot about the Plott breed and the storied individuals who made up the Big Five. Neader would routinely drive as many as six times a year from his Missouri home to visit the masters of the Plott breed back east. His devotion to the breed, to the hunt and to the history of the hound alone make Neader an important part of Plott dog history. But all of his other accomplishments are surpassed by the role he played in a historical Plott breed summit meeting that took place in 1963.

On February 23, 1963, Neader drove to West Virginia and picked up eighty-two-year-old Plott hound icon Isaiah Kidd. They headed south to Von Plott's farm in Plott Valley. It was here that they met some other big names in the Plott hound world to rewrite

Three-month-old Plott pup bred by Bud Lyon with Von Plott lineage.

the official standard for the breed. Von Plott and Isaiah Kidd were dissatisfied with the UKC and NPHA standards, especially their ommission of the buckskin Plott, and decided to correct their mistake. They invited other top names in the game, like Ross Snoake of Plymouth, Indiana, Joe Lukas of Ohio, Kenny Wells of Saluda, Virginia, Robert Daughtery of Lexington, Ohio, and Neader of Cape Girardeau, Missouri. These golden age Plott dog advocates spent almost two days discussing and hammering out how they felt the breed that they all loved so much should be accurately represented. Perhaps more importantly, the group actually had the foresight to preserve the history of the Plott dog lineage before it was too late to do so. By the time they were finished, they had provided the framework for the APA and AKC standard used today.

It would be more than twenty years before their efforts—later aided by John Jackson—paid off. But thanks to them, the original standards of the old-time Plott dog are preserved today. This meeting was not only one of great historical significance to the breed, but it was a poignant one as well. According to Neader, upon completion of the meeting, Von Plott honored his old friend Kidd by presenting him with a gift. The gift was a walking stick that Von's father, Plott patriarch Montraville Plott, had once owned. Kidd was moved to tears by this generous gesture and treasured the staff the remainder of his life.

By the late 1960s, the popularity of the Plott hound had spread farther up the eastern seaboard to include the northeastern states of America. As early as 1935, "Yankees" like Branch Rickey and others had come south to hunt and buy Plott hounds. Since that time many other citizens of the region have joined Rickey on their quest for the perfect hunt and the perfect dog, but none more famous than the legendary A.L. "Cheyenne" Hill of Center Conway, New Hampshire.

Hill grew up a seasoned hunter and outdoorsman, and he learned the value of hunting dogs at an early age. After serving in the marines during the Korean War, the rugged Hill returned home to New England to begin his career as a hunting guide and contract hunter. In the 1960s he opened the Dundee Mountain Guide service. He also did contract hunting work for local farmers.

Hill received his first Plott hounds from Sam George and has been a dedicated champion of the Plott hound breed ever since. Hill would later obtain Plott dog stock from his close friend Ellet Bias, who he hunted with as well. So Hill started at the top of the food chain with his first Plott dogs. All his stock had roots with four of the five members of the Big Five: Von Plott, Taylor Crockett, Isaiah Kidd and Gola Ferguson. And it would only get better from there. Over the next several decades he continued to run his hunting business with the help of his son Dennis, a U.S. Army Special Forces soldier, who later would become a licensed hunting guide in Alaska. If there was rogue varmint of any kind harassing any New Englander, Cheyenne Hill was the man who got the call to exterminate or catch it—and he always did.

As Hill's business and notoriety grew, so did his Plott pack. With his connections to Bias and George, he was able to keep his Plott dog bloodlines pure and strong. Hill also became a well-respected dog trainer, willing to do whatever it took to get the best out of his dogs when training them. He sometimes would imitate a bear while training his young Plott pups to give the dogs a taste of fighting and stalking a bigger "animal." His results spoke for themselves. Hill annually brought in record-setting big game totals for both himself and his customers, and he was a proud winner of the NPHA Methven Big Game Award. In his later years, Cheyenne Hill has remained an active and respected guide and hunter. He also has written some fine articles on his various hunting adventures along the eastern seaboard.

By 1980, the golden age of the Plott hound had passed. Four of the Big Five were dead. Only Taylor Crockett remained to carry the torch for the old guard of Plott hound history, and the old war horse carried it magnificently for sixteen more years. The Plott hound franchise was stronger than ever, as he and other advocates of the breed were now literally spread from coast to coast, from the original southern mountain empire across the heartland and throughout the Southwest. From the Rockies to the Pacific Northwest and all along the West Coast, the Plott hound was finally gaining recognition as the best big game hunting dog in America.

Yet there were those who questioned whether the legacy of the Plott hound could continue into the twenty-first century when all of the Big Five were gone. Just as importantly, there were those who would speculate as to the long-term future of the

Isaiah Kidd on left with Von Plott at Von's home on February 23, 1963, taking a break from a "Plott hound standards summit meeting."

Plott hound when these more contemporary advocates of the Big Five—these later-day golden age legends like Brandenburger, Bounds, Weems, Bowen, Jones, Methven, George, Bias, Hill and others—retired or passed on.

Who would carry the torch for them? It was a legitimate question. And it was one that was quickly answered.

Chapter Ten

CARRYING THE TORCH

In 1977, John Jackson, a young schoolteacher from Boone, North Carolina, made a purchase that would permanently change his life. Jackson, a native son of the southern mountains, already was an expert hunter and outdoorsman and an avid history buff. He inherited his love of reading and history from his parents, who were both career educators. Jackson was in the market for some hunting dogs and in doing his research became fascinated with the Plott hound breed. He first contacted Berlin King and ordered two Plott pups from him. This would be his first step toward becoming a modern-day torchbearer for the legacy of the Plott hound. In his further quest for knowledge of the breed, Jackson had learned of Dale Brandenburger, and he later ordered some pups from the golden age legend. Jackson was now convinced that the Plott hound was the right dog for him. Yet there was still something lacking, something missing, even in these fine Plott hounds, which he still could not quite put his finger on.

Yet, he forged on and rabidly began to research the breed. He visited Plott Valley where he met Bill and Larry Plott, as well as other Plott family descendants. He hungrily devoured every morsel of information that they, and others, shared with him. Jackson joined the NPHA and subscribed to as many hunting hound publications as he could afford. He visited, wrote and/or called most of the surviving pioneers of the golden age of the Plott breed so that he could pick their brains. All the while, John ardently hunted his Plott hounds, further honing his hunting skills. Jackson also studied dog breeding books to refine his animal husbandry abilities and further increase his canine knowledge.

Jackson carefully examined and studied old land grant records and wills, as well as other historical documents and letters, in order to learn more about his dogs and Plott family history. More importantly, unlike many young men, Jackson was smart enough to humble himself to the elder masters of the game so that he could learn from them. These old warriors appreciated a young man who was willing to do that and gladly took him under their wing. In doing so, he found exactly what he felt was lacking in his dogs—the traits of the old-time Plott hound. Jackson's challenge then became to find out if there were any of these old-time dogs still around, and if so, where he could get them.

As monumental an experience as getting his first Plott hound in 1977 was, it paled in comparison to another life-altering encounter that would take place in 1980. It was then that Jackson met and became the protégé of the last surviving member of the Big Five—the illustrious champion of the old-time Plott hound, Taylor Crockett. It was Crockett who would provide the answers to what John felt was lacking in his Plott hounds. And it was Crockett who would provide him actual examples of the old-time Plott dog.

Jackson gathered his courage and called the seventy-two-year-old Crockett, who graciously invited John to visit him at his job as a nightwatchman in Franklin, North Carolina. The two formed an immediate bond, almost instantly becoming friends, and this set the stage for Jackson to become a torchbearer for the old-time Crockett-Plott hound. On February 13, 1983, Jackson received his first Crockett-Plotts and from that point forward, he would keep no other type of Plott dog. This would be the start of his Little Elk Crockett-Plott hound kennels. John had finally been rewarded in his quest for knowledge of the old-time Plott hound.

For the next sixteen years Jackson would travel frequently to Crockett's Macon County home to learn at the knee of the old-time master. The two men would often hunt together, with Jackson never ceasing to be amazed at the strength and stamina of his elderly mentor. John would also form close bonds with other modern-day advocates of the breed—elder statesmen like Lawrence Porterfield, Robert Whitehead, Clyde Bounds and L.M. Moffett, as well as other younger men of the era, such as Jay Dorsey, another Crockett devotee. The wisdom he gained from all these resources, along with his own research, would result in Jackson becoming a fountain of information on the Plott hound breed. He quickly became known as the "go to"guy for anyone seeking information on the Plott hound or Plott history in general.

It was during this time that Jackson would play another key role in the saga of the Plott hound when he helped form the American Plott Association, or APA. On May 24, 1987, a dedicated group of Plott hound men met in Sweetwater, Tennessee, to discuss the formation of another national club to better promote the Plott hound. Clyde Neader was elected as the first president of the group; Harold Rice was voted vice-president; and John Jackson was elected as secretary and treasurer.

After electing officers, and drafting organizational bylaws, the newly founded group set about addressing the infamous omission of the buckskin Plott hound from the UKC and NPHA standards. These charter members wisely chose to reinstate the buckskin Plott to their own breed standard and elected to have their standard affiliated with the American Kennel Club, which allowed buckskins. The group also discussed ways to ensure that no outside infusions were allowed to unfairly skew the number of buckskins or dilute the pure Plott hound lineage.

But first, the group needed to carefully and articulately document their constitutional bylaws and official breed standards. The club knew exactly what they desired, but the challenge would be to eloquently and correctly record these goals in the most presentable manner. Without these operational guidelines and breed standards, the APA was doomed to fail. The preservation of the old-time Plott hound depended on their efforts to do this correctly.

The group wisely assigned club Secretary Jackson this monumental task. Clyde Neader suggested that Jackson use the breed guidelines that were first formulated in the February 1963 meeting held at Von Plott's home as his baseline standard. Jackson then set about rewriting them in a presentable manner that the American Kennel Club (or AKC) would find acceptable. After several months of hard work, John presented his project to the APA, which quickly ratified it and presented it to the AKC.

The APA had to then basically follow the same previously described steps as the NPHA did in 1946 with the UKC. The American Plott Association had to submit their breed standard to the AKC to get conditional recognition as foundation stock. The AKC approved this in 1987, and the buckskin was again part of the AKC and APA breed standard. But it would be more than a decade later, in 2004, before the APA would gain official AKC recognition as the parent club for the Plott hound breed. This guaranteed permanent official recognition of the old-time Plott hound and was a red-letter day in Plott dog history. Here is the AKC and APA Plott hound standard:

AMERICAN KENNEL CLUB PLOTT STANDARD

GENERAL APPEARANCE:
A hunting hound of striking color that traditionally brings big game to bay or tree, the Plott hound is intelligent, alert and confident. Noted for stamina, endurance, agility, determination and aggressiveness when hunting, the powerful, well-muscled, yet streamlined Plott combines courage with athletic ability.

SIZE, PROPORTION, SUBSTANCE:
Size-Height: Males—20 to 25 inches at the withers: Females—20 to 23 inches at the withers. Proportion: General conformation and height in proportion. Faults: Extremely leggy or close to the ground. Weight: (In hunting conditions) Males—50 to 65 pounds. Females—40 to 55 pounds. Substance: Moderately boned. Strong, yet quick and agile. Faults: Overdone. Carrying too much weight and/or too much bone to display speed and dexterity.

HEAD:
Head: Carried well up with skin fitting moderately tight. Faults: Folds, dewlap, skin stretched too tightly. Expression: Confident, inquisitive, determined. Faults: Sad expression. Eyes: Brown or hazel, prominent rather than deeply set. Faults: Drooping eyelids, red haw. Ears: Medium length, soft textured, fairly broad, set moderately high to high. Hanging gracefully with the inside part rolling forward toward the muzzle. Ear spread in males—18 to 20 inches. Ear spread in females—17 to 19 inches. When attentive or inquisitive, some Plotts display a semi-erectile power in their ears and lift them enough so a noticeable crease occurs on line with the crown. Disqualification: Length of ear extending beyond the tip of the nose or hanging bloodhound-like in long pendulous fashion. Skull: Moderately flat. Rounded at the crown with sufficient width between and above the eyes. Faults: Narrow-headed, square, oval or excessively dome.

John Jackson with his Crockett-Plotts, Hammer on left
and Queen.

Muzzle: Squared, pointed. *Pigmentation:* Eye rims, lips and nose are black. *Flews:* Black. Faults: Pendulous flews. *Bite-Teeth:* Scissors. Faults: Overshot or undershot.

NECK, TOPLINE AND BODY:

Neck: Meduim length, graceful, muscular and sloping. Clean and free of ponderous dewlap. Faults: Loose, wrinkled or folded skin. *Topline:* Gently sloping, slightly higher at the withers than at the hips. Faults: Roached. *Body-Chest:* Deep. *Ribs:* Deep. Moderately wide, well sprung. *Back:* Well muscled, strong, level. *Loin:* Gracefully arched. *Tail:* Root is slightly below level of topline. Rather long, carried free, well up, saber-like. Moderately heavy in appearance and strongly tapered. Sometimes typified by a slight brush.

FOREQUARTERS:

Shoulders: Clean, muscular and sloping, indicating speed and strength. *Elbows:* Squarely set. *Forelegs:* Straight, smooth, well muscled. *Pasterns:* Strong and erect. *Feet:* Firm, tight, well padded and knuckled, with strong toes. Set directly under the leg. Disqualification: Splayed feet. *Nails:* Usually black, although shades of reddish brown matching the brindle body color are permissible and buckskin colored dogs have light red nails. May be white when portions of the feet are white.

HINDQUARTERS:

Angulation: Well bent at stifles and at hocks. *Hips:* Smooth, round, and proportionally wide, indicating efficient propulsion. *Legs:* Long and muscular from hip to hock. From hock to pad—short, strong and at right angles to the ground. *Upper and Second Thigh:* Powerful and well muscled. *Feet:* Set back from under the body. Firm and tight. *Toes:* Strong.

COAT:

Smooth, fine, glossy, but thick enough to provide protection from wind and water. Rare specimens are double coated with a short, soft, thick inner coat concealed by a longer, smoother and stiffer outer coat.

COLOR:

Any shade of brindle (a fine streaked or a striped pattern of dark hair on a lighter background, or light streaks or stripes on a dark background) is preferred. This includes the following brindle factors: yellow, buckskin, tan, brown, chocolate, liver, orange, red, light or dark gray, blue or Maltese, dilute black brindle and black brindle. Other acceptable colors are black, brindle with black saddle, and black with brindle trim. A rare buckskin, devoid of any brindle, sometimes appears among litters, ranging from red fawn, sandy red, light cream, and yellow ochre, to dark fawn and golden tan. Some white on chest and feet is permissable, as is a graying effect around the jaws and muzzle.

GAIT:

Dexterous and graceful, rhythmic footfall. With ample reach in front and drive behind, the Plott can easily traverse various terrains with agility and speed. Legs converge to single track at speed.

TEMPERAMENT:
Eager to please, loyal, intelligent, alert. Aggressive, bold and fearless hunter. Disposition generally even, but varies among strains, with a distinction sometimes appearing between those bred for big game and those bred as coonhounds.

Reprinted with permission from AKC and APA.

Like the NPHA, the APA eventually started its own breed and field day events, first in Tennessee, and for the last several years near Rock Hill, South Carolina. Again, with the help of John Jackson, the club would also develop their own annual yearbook, called the *APA Brindle Book*. Over time the club would present numerous annual big game and hall of fame awards for their accomplished members. Though some would view the two groups as rivals, most Plott dog enthusiasts chose to be members of both groups, and equally supported them both.

Over the course of the next twenty years, Jackson would serve in various offices of the APA, including two terms as its president, and he would be awarded the group's most prestigous awards, such as the Hunter's Hall of Fame, as well as the NPHA's 2006 Frank Methven Big Game trophy. Jackson would also become an accomplished columnist for *Full Cry* magazine, and serve as editor of the *APA Brindle Book* on numerous occasions. He also has annually contributed excellent historical and hunting articles to the *APA Yearbook* and other publications.

But even all these well-deserved accolades are minor when compared to Jackson's two biggest contributions to the preservation of the Plott hound breed. First is his steadfast devotion to the perpetuation of the old-time Crockett-Plott hound. When his dear friend Taylor Crockett died in 1996, Jackson took it upon himself to honor him by dedicating the remainder of his life to the preservation and perpetuation of the Crockett-Plott hound. Today, twelve of the thirteen Plott dogs in his Little Elk Kennels originate directly from Taylor Crockett stock. The bottom line is that he continues to produce some of today's best examples of old-time Crockett-Plott hounds. Dogs like Cricket, Missy, Hammer and Hootie would all surely bring a smile to the old master Crockett's craggy face.

Aside from Jackson, to the best of my knowledge, only Lawrence Porterfield, Jay Dorsey, M.G. Webb, Eric Beck and Kenny Shelton continue to carry the Crockett torch. By that I mean that their entire kennels are, or were, completely or mostly devoted to old-time Crockett-Plott stock. And they carry it magnificently. More than anything else, this would have made Taylor Crockett proud to know that his legacy lives on.

Jackson's other greatest contribution to the breed is the in-depth research and documentation that he has done to preserve Plott hound and Plott family history. This alone makes him worthy of note in any study of the Plott hound breed. John Jackson is, in my opinion, the most eminent historian of the Plott breed living today. Perhaps just as importantly, he always graciously, humbly and willingly shares his wealth of knowledge with anyone seeking his help. He is a wonderful spokesman and modern-day torch carrier for the Plott breed.

John Jackson with three of his best
Crockett-Plotts—Angel, Cricket and
Hootie—on a hog hunt.

John Jackson's Hootie as a pup.

John Jackson with Hootie, the Crockett-Plott with nine lives.

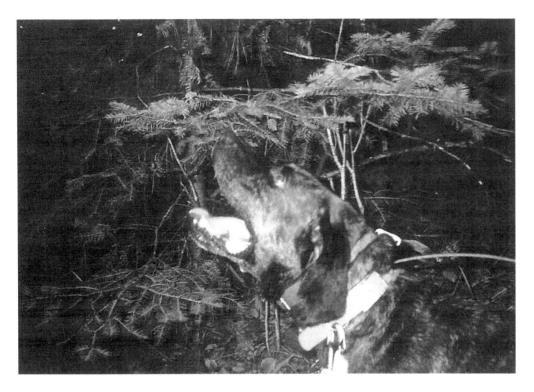

John Jackson's Cricket, one of his best Crockett-Plotts.

It was not too long after the APA was formed that the Plott hound received another unique honor, when it was named as the official state dog of North Carolina. This was due in large part to the efforts of a well-known family of the southern mountain empire—the Dillinghams. The Buncombe County, North Carolina community of Dillingham is named for some of the first pioneer settlers to the area. Lester Dillingham ran a general store in this picturesque mountain hamlet that was originally known as the Big Ivy. Lester obtained his first Plott hound directly from the Plott family in the 1940s and became a serious bear hunter. His store was a gathering place for local sportsmen to congregate and swap hunting stories and tips. Lester's son Hoyte was also a fine bear hunter and an early advocate of the Plott hound. He had his own pack of Plott dogs that he first registered in the 1950s, and Hoyte quickly proved himself a capable torchbearer for the Plott hound legacy.

Over the next forty years, Hoyte and his Plott hounds developed a stellar reputation, harvesting many a bear and winning numerous awards, including admission to the APA Hall of Fame. But of all his achievements in promoting the Plott breed, it is his work in getting the Plott hound recognized as the official state dog of North Carolina that he will be most celebrated for. Thanks to the tireless efforts of Hoyte Dillingham and other North Carolina Plott hound advocates, including Senator Robert Swain of Buncombe County and State Representative Charles Beale of Clyde, North Carolina, the state legislature named the Plott hound the official state dog of North Carolina on August 12,

1989. This was yet another star in the crown of the king (or queen) of big game hunting dogs—the Plott bear hound.

While John Jackson and Hoyte Dillingham were working to preserve the history of the breed and refining their own dog lines, still others were also carrying the torch for their golden age predecessors. Some prime examples include the previously mentioned Jay Dorsey of Blackstock, South Carolina, and North Carolinian Kenny Shelton, both staunch advocates of the Crockett-Plott dog.

It is somewhat ironic, but also fitting, that some of the young lions of the golden age—men like Bud Lyon, Jim Pfister, Robert Jones, Homan Fielder, Lawrence Porterfield, Robert Whitehead and Sam George, among others—have now all become senior spokesmen and torchbearers for the breed. It is very gratifying that these elder Plott dog pioneers are all graciously willing to serve as mentors and advisors to the current and future generations of Plott hound advocates. We are certainly blessed and fortunate to have these living examples of Plott hound history still working hard to support, promote and advance the breed.

A good example of children carrying the torch for their legendary fathers is that of Steve and David Fielder. Homan Fielder, a golden age era icon, instilled a love for the Plott breed in his sons at a very early age. Both Fielder lads would follow in their father's footsteps, perpetuating the Bear Pen line of Plott hounds begun by their father in the late 1950s. Steve Fielder in particular would become an exceptional spokesman for the Fielder clan, as well as the Plott hound breed. Steve was born in 1946 and with the exception of a stint in the military, he has spent his entire career working for nationally recognized kennel clubs such as the UKC, PKC and AKC. But at the same time, he has also helped his father and brother promote and hunt their Bear Pen Plott hounds. Steve's dog, Bear Pen Bronco, was the 1986 NPHA national champion. Bear Pen Plott hounds have won many other national and regional awards, and Fielder has served as president of the NPHA, among other numerous personal honors.

Steve is currently serving as assistant vice-president for AKC Coon Dog Events, and he travels the nation promoting the Plott breed in that position. Fielder also created what is widely recognized as the best online Plott hound resource—Plottdogs.com. This website is easily accessible and attractive, with a wealth of Plott hound information, as well as forums for visitors to "talk Plotts."

David Fielder has kept a lower profile than his more recognized brother, staying closer to home. But he too has played an integral role in the Fielder family Plott hounds—breeding, training and hunting the remarkable Bear Pen Plotts. Homan Fielder, now eighty-seven years old, remains an active senior statesman for the Plott hound and surely is proud of his sons and how they have continued his legacy. It is easy to see why the Fielder family is held in such high regard in the Plott hound world.

Fielder's West Virginia neighbor, Sam George of White Sulphur Springs, shares his pride in how his family carries on his line of fine Plott hounds. Sam's daughter, Lisa Johnson, is very knowledgeable about Plott hound history and the breed in general. She and her husband Ricky, as well as their son Nathaniel, help Sam take care of his dogs today. Sam—still an active hunter at age seventy-one—has passed his skills on to young Nathan, who already has been in on several bear kills and won

C.E. "Bud" Lyon with pup from his latest litter of seventh-generation Von Plott lineage.

Steve Fielder with his Plott hound Shooter at 2007 APA Breed Days.

the APA 2006 Young Coonhunter of the Year Award. And the lad is still several years away from his sixteenth birthday!

Rodney Burris Jr. can take a page from the Fielder and George family traditions, as he continues to learn from his father, current APA President Rodney Burris Sr. The senior Burris, though still a young man himself, became a Plott breed authority when he started his Benton, Tennessee Hillside Kennels. Burris and his Hillside Plott hounds quickly gained recognition as accomplished coon and big game hunters in the South and Midwest. Hillside Plotts come from a variety of excellent bloodlines, but primarily derive from the Demoss Cascade Plott lineage. Rod Junior proved to be a quick study to his dad, as he has won many coon dog competitions and proudly carries on the Burris family Plott dog legacy. Rod Senior should be proud of both his family and dogs, as well as the fine leadership he has demonstrated as the current presiding officer of the APA.

Right over the mountain from the Burris family, in Robbinsville, North Carolina, lives another dynamite father-son Plott dog duo, Roy and Robert Stiles. While working toward his master's degree in chemistry at Western Carolina University, Roy roomed with the Ferguson family and was exposed firsthand to Plott hound living history. He caught "the Plott hound bug" early and would eventually start his own Plott hound kennel, actively hunting his dogs in the Carolinas, Georgia, Michigan, Canada and Wisconsin. The Stiles family now has more than forty Plott hounds, mostly derived from Everette Weems, Von Plott and Gola Ferguson bloodlines. Roy got two of his first Plott hounds from Larry Plott and Bud Lyon. Recently he has sent twenty-eight of his Plott hounds to Germany where they are used to hunt boar, yet another indicator of the fine reputation of his pack. Stiles subscribes to the old-time breeding theory and therefore will not breed any of his Plotts until they have been proven "woods worthy." By that he means that they must have performed well on a hunt before he will breed them. He also specifically trains his Plotts on either bear or boar—but never both—as he feels that they require specific skills and temperaments for each. Roy has served six times as APA president and has represented the Plott breed well. His son Robert is poised to carry on the family Plott hound tradition, as he won the 2003 APA Young Big Game Hunter Award, and his dog Hammer was named the 2006 APA Coon Dog of the Year.

Other dynamic East Coast supporters of the breed include Richard and Chase Hope, Duane Smith, Eddie Hoge, Eugene Walker, George and Marge Robinson, Gene White, Archie Boone and R.C. Roarke. They are joined by Marion and Kay Allison, Jerome and Carol Barr, Richard Martin and Burdet Brinkley, all of whom proudly carry on the East Coast Plott hound tradition.

But, just as in the golden age, these modern-day Plott proponents were not limiting themselves to just perpetuating the breed, which was important, but they were also working on improving it. Plott people like Charles Gantte not only proudly carried the Plott hound torch, but also refined it. Near the end of the golden age era, Gantte, of Dandridge, Tennessee, set about creating his own strain of Plott hound. Gantte is a well-educated man, having studied both genetics and biology extensively while in college, and he put that education to good use in the development of the Gantte-Plott hound.

Gantte started with prime Hack Smithdeal and Gola Ferguson Plott hound foundation stock, and over the next thirty years he worked feverishly to refine it. By the end of the twentieth century, these long-legged, mostly dark-colored, cold-nosed, hyperaggressive canines became the rage of the Plott dog world. For five to six years near the end of the millennium, the Gantte-Plotts proved to be nearly unbeatable in bear bay competitions across the nation. And they were superb big game dogs in the field, too. Some of Gantte's best-known dogs include, among others, Minnie, Tug, Bowser and Smoky Mountain Jeff. Surely the old master Plott breeder Gola Ferguson would have been proud to see his original Plott dog stock not only preserved but also improved upon. Today, folks like Roger Botkin and Dick McCoy in West Virginia and Wayne McCurry of North Carolina carry the torch for both Plott hound innovators—Gola Ferguson and Charles Gantte.

In the Midwest, the modern-day Plott hound torch burns brighter than ever. Thanks to, among others, Jim Schwinefus, Lynn Sires, Joe Polly, George Weber, Eddie Weber, Chad Barth, Rex Meinert, Jim Wanta, Jay Waeltz and Dave Trumbo, the Midwest remains a stronghold for Plott hounds. Breed enthusiasts from the past and present can rest assured that our torch is being carried in the Midwest.

Washington state, once known as a hotbed for hunting with Plott hounds, and home to many legends of Plott dog history, has unfortunately recently outlawed bear hunting with dogs. Increases in human population and decreases in open hunting lands have also adversely affected the opportunity to hunt with hounds in the West. Yet the Plott hound continues to be a force in the region, thanks in part to senior statesman Frank Methven and torch carrier Gordon Larson.

Today, at age eighty-seven, Frank Methven is nearing completion of his third book and remains an inspiration to anyone interested in Plott hounds. Few, if any, individuals can legitimately make the claim to have known and/or hunted with most of the past and present-day Western legends of Plott hound history. But Frank Methven can, and he is a humble, but much celebrated breed icon himself. And rightly so.

Gordon Larson lived in various locations growing up, but as an adult he moved to Washington state primarily to hunt bear with his Plott dogs. In 1961 Larson obtained his first Plotts from Stuart Sharret, another early Western breed pioneer. Of course, like most Western Plott hounds, they derived originally from Von Plott stock. But Larson's dogs got a double dose of this legendary bloodline when North Carolinian Roy Stiles later infused additional Von Plott stock, along with Weems and Ferguson bloodlines, into the Larson hounds.

No less an expert than 2006 Frank Methven Award winner John Jackson believes Gordon Larson is probably one of the top ten bear hunters in the United States. Jackson adds:

Gordon Larson is a dedicated, intelligent and experienced hunter and Plott hound man. But, while there are others who share those qualities, Gordon is different in that he is a student of the sport and the dog—he studies them. He always is learning and honing his skills. He knows his prey. He knows their habits. He can think like they can and anticipate what their next moves will be. Just as importantly, perhaps more so, he can read a dog. He can look at one and just know what to expect from it. That is a rare talent that few possess. Plus, he knows how to evaluate a dog too, to quickly identify a top-grade hound. Gordon is a great judge of people and dogs. One of the best I have ever seen.

Larson is a staunch advocate of staying true to the breed and not outcrossing his Plotts with inferior strains. Perhaps best of all, he realizes and appreciates the history of the breed. As he states in the 2006 *APA Brindle Book*: "The Plott hound has proven to me to be the best bear-hunting dog available today. The original Plotts were superior bear dogs and worked well on other game too. Because those original dogs are part of American history, heritage and culture, I think we have a duty to keep the Plott as it was intended by our forefathers—a true mountain bear dog. If it ain't broke, don't fix it!"

Amen, Mr. Larson. Well said.

Another intriguing Western frontman for the Plott hound is Idaho's George Ricks. Though now approaching seventy years old, George Ricks can still outrun hunters half his age, usually being the first man to get to the bear. But as skilled an outdoorsman as he is—and he is one of the best—it is his dedication to the old-time Plott hound and to refining his own strain of Plott dog that is his most impressive achievement. Though he has lived in Idaho most of his life, Ricks is a North Carolina native, hailing originally from Cherokee, North Carolina. Like golden age–era pioneer Rickey Red Eagle, Ricks is of Cherokee descent.

The Ricks family, like a lot of North Carolinians, left their mountain home in search of work after World War II. Many of these rugged outdoorsmen often found work in Western logging camps, and in many cases took their Plott hounds with them to their new homes and jobs. George Ricks was no different. He took his family and Plott hounds to find work in Idaho, where he still lives today. With so much big game in the region, George Ricks and his Plott hounds took to the area like a duck to water. But unlike most Western Plott hounds, his dogs came directly from the East Coast, with no stops in the Midwest, and are more like the old-time Plott hounds described in Chapter Six.

The original Ricks-Plott hound probably came from the stock of Rickey Red Eagle, who was one of the first folks to register his Plott dogs in the late 1940s. His first registered Plott was Red Eagle's Doctor C, who was whelped from two of his other top hounds, Ruff and Rebel. The Indians in the Smokies seemed to appreciate the appeal of the old-time Plott dogs better than most. These Cherokee Plotts were rough, raw-boned, aggressive, multipurpose dogs of the highest order. And that's where the George Ricks–Plott hound strain began.

As Ricks grew into manhood, becoming a skilled hunter and Plott dog breeder, he not only recognized the value of his family Plott hounds, but also worked to preserve and improve them. He was not interested in fame, awards or registration papers—only results. Ricks realized that the best way to get those results was to linebreed and inbreed his pack, keeping only the best of the best and culling the rest—no exceptions. He took this approach very seriously and strictly adhered to these guidelines. He would tolerate no foolishness of any kind in his pursuit of the preservation and refinement of the old-time Ricks-Plott hounds. George Ricks's approach to his dogs is very similar to that taken by the original Plott family, as they worked for over two hundred years to preserve and protect their lineage, allowing only the best outside breed infusions. And it is the same approach taken by his Eastern Cherokee tribe, which also took the traditional steps in keeping their Plott dog lineage as pure as possible.

After almost half a century of hard work, the results speak for themselves. These Ricks-Plott hounds are excellent tracking dogs, yet run to their prey with their heads up, fast on the track and full of intelligence, all marks of an aggressive, old-time Plott dog. Just as described in Chapter Six, they are not as "houndy" in appearance, and vary in color, but epitomize all the best qualities of the old-time Plott hound. The Ricks-Plott hounds, though true old-time Plotts, differ a bit in appearance from the Crocketts, yet are some of the best examples we have today of the old-time Cherokee Plott stock. At the same time, thanks to Ricks's hard work over the past fifty years, the old-time Cherokee stock has not only been preserved, but also refined. That is the ultimate compliment to an expert dog breeder.

Though he has no interest in registration papers, some of George's favorite Plott hounds, based on grit, tenacity and most importantly, results, include Sara, Buddy and Blackie. George's good friend and hunting partner, Idaho logger Randy Zumwalt, also keeps prime examples of Ricks-Plott stock. It is interesting to mention that while most notable Plott hounds migrated from the East to the West—as did the original Ricks dogs—today's refined strain of Western Ricks Plotts are now finding homes on the East Coast.

Today, friends of George Ricks, such as Charles Smith of Lenoir, North Carolina, Eddie Frizell of Black Mountain, North Carolina, and Dan Johnson of Morganton, North Carolina—all good bear hunters and Ricks-Plott dog owners—now proudly carry the torch for the Ricks-Plott hounds. It seems a sort of poetic justice that the Plott hound has come full circle, with a refined strain of old-time dog returning to its original North Carolina mountain home, while George Ricks continues to bring fame to the breed in the far west.

I think it is safe to say that the Plott hound masters of the golden age, as well as the original patriarchs of the dog, can rest assured that the breed has been well preserved across the nation, and even around the world. Their torches have been carried—and carried well—into the twenty-first century.

Now let's take a look at what helped make the Plott breed famous—hunting the black bear.

Chapter Eleven

HUNTING THE BLACK BEAR

No history of the Plott hound would be complete without at least some discussion of hunting the black bear. Over the years the Plott dog and the sport of bear hunting have become almost synonymous. Though the Plott hound has proven itself to be a superb multipurpose hunting dog, it was bear hunting that would bring worldwide fame to the breed.

Bear hunting with Plott hounds began in the eighteenth century as a matter of survival—protecting families and farms and putting food on the table. Today it has evolved into a "sport." But whether for survival or sport, it remains extremely challenging, though the basic hunting and dog training techniques have changed little in almost three centuries. And even though the Plott hound has evolved over the years—some say for the better, others for the worse—the specific traits and skills needed for a top-notch Plott bear dog also remain the same. This is what—then and now—makes the breed so unique.

But there are areas in which bear hunting has drastically changed over the years. Obviously weapons, transportation, communications and tracking collar devices, as well as a reduction in game lands, have all greatly impacted the sport. For example, old-time hunters used a hunter's horn to call their dogs in or signal them to their location. This was basically a large cow horn, similar to the powder horn used with muzzleloading rifles, except in this case both ends were open. With practice, the old-timers could not only get a loud sound from blowing into the horn, but one that was uniquely theirs, that their dogs would recognize and return to.

Today, in an effort to prevent their hounds from being stolen or lost, hunters use radio tracking collars on their dogs. Some even have electronic chips embedded under the animal's skin to aid in locating the hound. Tracking collars did not come into use until the late 1960s, when Clyde Bounds and others helped develop them. Since then, they have become a vital part of hound hunting gear. Two-way radios and cellphones also aid hunters in communicating with each other and in locating their dogs as well as their prey.

Modern firearms are a big improvement over the single-shot black powder guns of the past, in that they rarely misfire or malfunction and can be fired several times without reloading. This has made for more humane and efficient kills, as well as improved hunter safety.

Old-time hunters hunted by foot and on horseback. They worked and lived in the outdoors daily and knew the region intimately. For instance, in the late 1800s, Montraville Plott would often leave his home in Plott Valley on horseback, without his dogs, and head northwest about ten miles to the Black Rock area of the Qualla Boundary. He knew this to be a good hunting area and would set up a base camp there. Mont's wife Julia would release a few of his Plott hounds at a pre-arranged time after his leaving, usually the next day. These superbly trained canines not only would head straight to him, but also, as soon as they found him, they would strike a bear trail and the hunt was on. Hunts back then could last a week or more, or as long as it took to "make meat."

Today's hunts are usually shorter, a few days or less. Hunting seasons are also not as long today, and there are fewer hunting lands available. Dogs and hunters are usually transported to the hunting site in trucks, SUVs or four-wheelers, though the actual hunting is still done on foot.

Over the years the number of dogs on the hunt has changed too. Most experts agree that five to eight dogs are adequate, but today sometimes up to fifteen or more may come along, or as many as each hunter can handle and care for. In the past there were seldom more than a few dogs on a hunt, depending on the size of the hunting party, the reason being that most hunters of that era could not afford to keep more than a few Plotts on their farms. It was simply too expensive to feed them. The commercial dog food that is so commonly available today was unheard of then. A staple food for both humans and Plott hounds in the mountain empire was corn bread. It was common for mountain folks back then to bake fine-grained corn bread for their family—and a cheaper, coarse-grained cake of corn bread for their dogs. Corn bread and table scraps were all the dogs had to eat. Von Plott told of once being on a bear hunt when the only food left for both hunters and hounds was corn bread. He said that it was so cold that the corn bread had frozen and that his party had to break it up for the dogs by stomping it on a log.

Yet for all these differences, today's bear hunters and their Plott hounds share many similarities with their old-time predecessors. Hunters, then and now, generally first scout their desired hunting area to determine if game is in the region. Once "bear sign" has been found, the hunters return to the area with their Plott hounds and the hunt begins.

Before going further, we should first examine the specific elements of the bear hunt and the exact roles played by the Plott hound in it. Initially the hunters usually separate into two groups—standers and drivers. The drivers do just that; with the help of the Plott hounds they ideally drive the bear to the standers. The standers usually are strategically placed at various locations, often several miles away where the bear is anticipated to run to.

Sometimes Plott dogs are placed with the standers too, in order to add fresh dogs and increase pressure to the chase as the bear passes. In some cases though, the stander will kill the bear as it passes. Other times the dogs will "bay" or tree the bear before it passes the stander and the drivers make the kill. The Plott hounds play several well-defined roles on the bear hunt. They are, for the most part, specialized in six different categories—strike, start, trail, pack, bay and catch dogs. But most Plotts possess at least some of all these skills, though catch dogs are usually used only for hog hunting.

The strike dog is a more cold-nosed Plott hound, with superior tracking or trailing skills and the ability to find a trail on its own. The strike dog is so well trained that it will trail or run *nothing* but bear. The strike dog (or dogs) is released first to establish a definite bear trail. Once the trail has been found, the start, trail and pack dogs, as well as still later, the bay dogs, are released.

The start dog has the similar cold-nosed traits of the strike dog, but their nose is not as highly refined. Therefore, it seldom will find bear sign on its own. Instead the hunter must take the start dog to the sign, and the start dog begins to trail from there. If both strike and start dogs are on the hunt, the hunter will release the strike dog first to firmly establish the bear trail, and the start dog second to reenforce it. The hunters/drivers follow these dogs, accompanied by the rest of the pack, with leads still on, as closely as possible.

The trail and pack dogs are the next hounds released. Now that the bear trail has been firmly established, the drivers will release their trail dogs one at a time, in intervals to continue trailing the bear. The trail hounds are known as "warm-nosed" dogs in that they have some tracking or trailing skills, but are not as highly developed as the strike or start hounds. These dogs are still trailing by scent and don't "run over" it as the more aggressive pack and bay dogs often do.

The drivers then release the pack dogs to join the hunt. A pack dog is blessed with speed and stamina and will generally run over the scent or track in their pursuit of both the other Plotts and the bear. The pack dogs are "fed" or released in intervals too, in order to increase pressure on the bear as it is being chased. This is also known as "packing the trail." By adding pack hounds to the chase it adds more excitement, or "dog power," to the race.

The hunters can eventually tell by the baying of their hounds how close the dogs are to the bear, or if the bruin is slowing down to fight or tree. The hunters then release the last hounds in the pack—the bay dogs. The bay dogs (also known as catch dogs in hog hunting) are usually not good trailing dogs and have a more aggressive temperament. The bay dog's job is to bay or contain the bear while it is treed or on the ground.

Though each of these dogs plays a specialized role in the hunt, they all often share many of the same skills. Some strike, trail and pack dogs are good fighters; some bay dogs have good trailing skills. However, for the most part the dogs' specific skills are identified early on by their owner and they are used accordingly. Nevertheless, having all or even some of these skills is what makes the Plott hound so special. But for all their many attributes, the Plotts are probably best known for their tenacious, gritty big game "fighting" skills.

Speaking of fighting, it should be noted that the Plott hound's style of "fighting" a bear and a hog are distinctly different. In hog hunting, the bay or catch dog's objective is to do just that—catch or latch onto the hog by biting either its ears or rear legs to contain the hog until the hunter can make the kill. It would be suicide for a Plott hound to try this when bear hunting. The bruin just has too large a size and strength advantage. Therefore, the objective in bear hunting is for the bay dog to bay the bear by either treeing it or by containing it while on the ground until the hunter intervenes, hence the term "bay."

Like the catch dog, the bay dog must be brave and aggressive. But unlike the catch dog, the bay dog's job is to contain the bear by barking, nipping or feinting at it, *not* by biting or holding onto the animal. Containing the bear, but staying just out of the bruin's kill range until the hunter arrives, is the primary goal of the bay dog. Anything else almost always results in injury or death to the hound.

Good bloodlines will help ensure most of these attributes, while temperament and "nose" will determine the rest. But the ultimate deciding factor regarding the hound's specific role is how it performs on the game trail. However, to best prepare the Plott dog for this, most experts use a few well-established training methods. Von Plott, for instance, kept it pretty simple. He felt that his Plott hounds were born with hunting instincts and that it was simply their nature to do so. Von thought that all he needed to do initially was to try and determine which dogs were strike dogs and which were pack dogs. Of course, the problem here is that you never really know for sure how the dog will perform until you hunt with it. Sometimes the best-trained and best-looking dogs will fall short on a real-life bear hunt. Even after the best of training, the ultimate deciding factor as to determining a bay or strike dog is how they perform on the hunt.

Von's first training technique was to get the hounds used to game scent. Then, when the pups were about a year old, start them out with some other experienced dogs and get them in the woods often to hunt. Basic instincts would take care of the rest. He described his dog training methods and use of strike dogs in detail to some *Foxfire* staff members in 1976. Von elaborated as well on how one of his famous strike hounds—Blueboy— needed almost no training. He said:

> *I train my dogs when they're three or four months old—take 'em to the woods and let 'em learn what their nose is for. You take them out and find your bear track and you can tell whether he* [the dog] *is going to be ready or not when he smells it. It's up to the dogs. They train themselves. It's instinct. He knows what you want when he gets big enough. First bear he smells, he takes after it. He might go after a coon a little, but we usually lead 'em till we find a* [bear] *track and then turn 'em on it and they go right. But I don't actually let them get on a bear 'till they are older. When he gets about a year old, you can put him on a bear, but don't put him on any younger than that. He's a boy. He ain't a man yet. That's the way it runs you know? He's not got after one like an old dog. He'll have to be a year old before I put him on a bear.*
>
> *We put them in with experienced dogs so they can learn what to do. You use a strike dog—one that's had a lot of experience, you know—to find the bear, and then you turn the other ones loose. I had two strike dogs once* [that were so good] *I could go to the woods where the bear was, and I didn't even need to hunt a track. I could unsnap them, and if you heard one, you could turn the rest loose. He'd be on a bear. You have got to hunt them regular to get them like that. Main thing is you want to get your dogs all together*

The maltese-colored Blueboy, one of Von Plott's all-time best strike dogs.

when you turn them loose. Turn them loose together on a track, and they'll stay together. Then soon as the bear is killed, the dogs are put back on their leads right there…

[But some dogs don't need training.] *I had one dog once that was about fourteen months old when bear season opened. He wasn't really big enough that first year. So these fellers from over in Clay County was wanting me to come and kill a big bear. They were afraid of it. So I took this young dog, and the whole pack, but he was still the biggest and stoutest, about twenty-seven inches tall. He never smelt a bear before, but he smelt that bear and he just wanted to go. And you know what I done? I turned him loose as a strike dog. He ran over bushes as high as that window after that bear, and he never smelt one before. His name was Blueboy.*

C.E. "Bud" Lyon echoed Von's sentiments regarding Blueboy. Lyon told me in 2007 that Blueboy was perhaps the best strike dog he had ever seen. The dog just intuitively knew what to do when striking a bear trail. And the trail conditions did not matter. Blueboy was a true cold-nosed strike dog. No matter how old the trail was, he would find it every time and stay with it.

The Cable family was also well known as exceptional puppy trainers, but they used slightly different training techniques. They always started their Plott pups out baying groundhogs, raccoons and even cats. Once the pups were older and acclimated to trailing and hunting, they would graduate to the big game arena. Yet after the initial training period, most of the Cables would never use one of their hounds to hunt raccoons until it was older and retired from bear or boar hunting. I am not sure how they specifically trained the dogs to differentiate between the two, but they evidently did.

Old-time legend Quill Rose told authors Wilbur Zeigler and Ben Grosscup in their book *The Heart of the Alleghenies*, in 1883, that Plott men of his era had dog training down to a fine art. He added, "They keep three to eight hounds, who hold themselves strictly to their masters' orders. None needed to be yoked or leashed, and simply at his word, when a scent is sprung, one is ordered to follow alone. Shortly, another will be ordered to go, and so on, until all are released and on their own separate trail."

Quill differed a bit in his own approach on the hunt, as he kept two strike (or lead) dogs tied, and let them strike a trail one at a time in intervals, and then he released his three pack dogs to follow once the trail had been definitely established. Unfortunately Quill left few, if any, details as to what specific training methods he used to achieve this sort of well-disciplined Plott hound.

Modern-day hunter John Jackson takes a page from the Cable training manual and starts his Crockett-Plotts out on coons. To get a pup started properly, sometimes a raccoon is captured and put in a rolling cage to prevent it from injury, and the dogs can bay and tree it. Over time, as he learns more about his dogs, Jackson will decide if he wants to use them on big or small game. He has found that it is best to use them on one or the other, and he will rarely use a coon dog to hunt big game.

Training techniques vary for strike dogs, but most bear hunters I talked with used a similar, or the same, type of method as those described previously by Von Plott, the Cables and John Jackson. But like anything else, it is a combination of factors—not just one thing—that make for a superb hunting Plott hound: breeding, training, persistence and getting the dog in the woods *often*.

AKC Vice-president Steve Fielder feels that certain strains of Plott hounds are more suited for specific game than others. For instance, he feels that Crockett-Plotts are more aggressive and better suited as bay dogs for hunting bear, or catch dogs for boar, than some other Plott strains. Additionally, he thinks that some of the more "houndy" strains of Plotts, such as the later-day Von Plott lineage, are better trackers or strike dogs. Fielder also believes that you can hunt both small and big game with the same Plotts.

Others, like 2005 Methven winner Roy Stiles, are adamant that a top bear or big game hound should be used only for big game. Some hunters even take it further than that, specializing their big game dogs on either bear or boar—but not both. They feel that hunting too many types of game will confuse the dog and increase the potential for chaos on the hunt—the hound may choose to pursue small game instead of bear.

However, a similarity that both modern and old-time hunters share is a fierce devotion to their favorite Plott hounds. No one describes this better than Frank Methven. Methven's all-time favorite Plott hound, Battle Cry, was given to him by Von Plott. Battle Cry would become the best strike dog Methven ever owned. By the time he was three years old, Battle Cry had been on 107 bear kills and had hunted around the world. Unfortunately, he would not live to see his fourth birthday, as he went missing on a bear hunt during his third hunting season. Methven was devastated by the loss, and in 1979 he wrote a uniquely moving eulogy to his beloved dog, as well as to his recently deceased friend Von Plott. It was first printed in the 1979 *NPHA Yearbook* and reads in part like this:

> *Plott's Battle Cry is now with you, Mr. Von Plott, for you are the man responsible for his creation. Battle Cry was an outstanding strike dog from the rig since he was ten months of age; on the road, in the swamps, or along the rivers, streams, lakes or mountains, and was hunted with men and their dogs from over half the United States and several foreign countries. He was a proud dog, Mr. Plott. In his entire life he never put his feet upon any person nor licked the hand of any man. I wish he had. His allegiance to the man that fed him and hunted him was secondary. His sole dedication was to that of hunting bear. Battle Cry is with you now, Mr. Plott, as he was when he was a puppy. He will remember your voice. Speak to him of soft warm days and fresh clean streams, of clear blue skies and honest men's laughter. Talk to him of towering mountains, of winding rivers, of Plott voices that sound through the shadows of the night, and of the remembered winds of a legendary day. That was his heritage and the spirit of his heart. You gave Battle Cry to the bear dog hunting world, and he now returns to you from a brief life of achievement. I miss him, Mr. Plott, but I know you are pleased to have him and all the others with you. He bore your name proudly, Mr. Plott, and your knowing hand now rests upon his worthy head.*

If that doesn't show you how much hunters care for their dogs then nothing will.

In addition to being a skilled woodsman and devoted to his dogs, the truly outstanding hunter must have a fiery, unsurpassed passion for the hunt. This is what separates the merely good or average hunter from the great ones. Both the dog and their master simply live to hunt—it is in their blood—they are born with it. It is similar to how boxing trainers describe their world-class fighters. All the skills in the world are useless without the heart of a champion. That desire to compete and refusal to surrender is the essence of a true fighter. That can't be taught—you either have it or you don't. The same principles apply to Plott hounds and their masters. Taylor Crockett said it best in *Foxfire Five*:

> *Bear hunting with dogs is the most rugged sport we have in the hunting line. To do it right you have to be in good physical condition. You find the bear generally in the very roughest places that he can find. It calls for a lot of endurance and determination and perseverance. Just everybody's not a bear hunter. A real bear hunter likes to get in there with the dogs and find the track and turn loose on him. That separates the men from the boys is the old saying.*

Authors Wilbur Zeigler and Ben Grosscup pretty much summed it up when they visited with Israel "Wid" Medford, a renowned bear hunter, in his hunting camp about eight miles south of Waynesville, North Carolina, around 1881. Medford was nearly sixty-five then, but still a physical force and a rabid bear hunter. When asked if he loved bear hunting, Medford's two-word reply says it all. He simply exclaimed: "Good Law [Lord]!" He then elaborated further. When asked if he could live his life over, what

Frank Methven's dog Battle Cry, given to him by Von Plott. Battle Cry was in on 107 bear kills, until he went missing on a bear hunt at age three.

would he change, Wid replied, "I'd get me a neat woman and go to the wildest country in creation and hunt from the day I was big enough to tote a rifle gun, until old age and roomaticks fastened on me!"

Medford concluded, "Traps is good fer them that hunts rabbits, and rabbit hunting is good fer boys. But fer me, give me my old flintlock shooting iron and let a keen pack of lean hounds be hoppin' ahead. And of all sports, the master sport is following their music over the mountains and winding up with a bullet or sticker in a varminous old bear!"

Spoken like a man who is truly passionate about his sport, this is a trait shared by all the great hunters and hounds in Plott dog history. Many people who don't understand consider the sport barbaric and cruel to the dog. Nothing could be further from the truth. As John Jackson says, "There is a lot more to hunting than just killing something." And he is right. Hunters and hounds love the chase. They love being outdoors and enjoying nature. More importantly, hunters love their dogs and take pride in them, treating them like family. Certainly they both want a successful hunt, but at the end of the day, it is the hunt itself—not just the kill—that really matters to the true sportsman and their dogs. Steve Fielder said it best: "Just seeing a bear killed is never the reason we hunted."

The Plott hounds have been bred for almost three hundred years to hunt. They *need* to hunt. I have seen dogs in kennels or tied that when freed ran straight to the dog box on a truck and jumped in, when they just as easily could have run away. No, these magnificent animals are doing exactly what they were born to do and what they *want* to do.

As bear hunting with Plott hounds became more of a sport in the early twentieth century, hunts often became more challenging due to both the scarcity of game as well as a reduction of game lands. The bears that remained often became legends in their own right, as adversaries to the Plott hound. Some, in fact, became so famous for eluding the hunters and hounds for such a long time that they were given specific names to honor them. Bears like Old Kettlefoot, Old Reelfoot, Big Black or Honest John would all prove to be worthy foes to the Plott breed.

Seldom have two totally different animals shared such a rich and storied history as that of the Plott bear hound and the North American black bear. Both are uniquely different, but in other ways strangely the same. One, a domesticated German import, a dog whose lineage has been refined for over 250 years in its new American home, a hound fiercely devoted to, and protective of, its human master. The other, an American native, the uncivilized, natural king of the wilderness, who has become a fitting and fearless symbol for all that we love and respect about the great outdoors.

But both of these majestic animals have similar qualities too. They each are blessed with incredible stamina and a savage fighting spirit. Both carry themselves in a proud, regal manner, somehow innately knowing that they are each a rare and special breed. Perhaps most importantly, both are a primal connection to our primitive past, when most of our entire country was a new frontier. They are a reminder of what many feel were the good old days, when folks were self-sufficient and truly appreciated a hard, but simple and less complicated way of life. It is easy to understand how the Plott hounds and their owners would be proud to have the mighty bruin included in their name—the

Plott *bear* hound. It is even easier to see why these two amazing animals will be forever associated and honored together.

It is a fitting tribute to each of these amazing creatures that even with the encroachment of civilization and the complexities of modern life, both the Plott bear hound and their noble adversary, the black bear, continue to not only survive, but also thrive in the fast-paced world of the twenty-first century.

Now, let's close with a brief look at the Plott bear hound of today.

Chapter Twelve

NOTES AND MUSINGS ON THE PLOTT HOUND TODAY

Almost a decade into the new millennium—and more than 250 years after first arriving in America—the Plott bear hound continues to command respect as the premier big game hunting dog in the United States. While there are those who contend that the dog has deteriorated since the golden age of the breed, there can be no doubt that the Plott hound today is more popular than it has ever been. And for good reason.

A quick Internet search for the Plott hound produces more than 200,000 different websites with information relating to the Plott breed or pertaining to clubs, services and kennels. No fewer than seven states have formal, well-organized bear hunting organizations that are devoted to preserving the heritage of bear hunting with hounds. There are at least seven additional clubs that are dedicated to hunting with Plott hounds in some capacity. In addition, there are several different magazines published monthly or annually that are devoted to hunting with Plott hounds or dogs in general.

These numbers pale in comparison to the massive growth of the sport of raccoon or "coon" hunting with Plotts. Almost every state in the union now has some form of state and/or local club promoting coon hunting with Plott hounds, or with the other five breeds of coonhounds that are approved by the UKC and AKC. The AKC alone will put on more than 1,452 coon hunting–related competitions in 2007 and the UKC three times that many. Both clubs combined will put on more than 7,000 field events this year that Plott hounds are eligible for. (See definitions of field events and competitions in the Glossary.)

John Hagin, the great-nephew of APA charter member Robert Jones, is one of the many folks who is fiercely devoted to the sport of coon hunting with Plotts and who participate in these competitions. But Hagin has taken his interest in the sport to a whole new level, and in doing so he has done something that has never been done before. Hagin, a twenty-five-year-old schoolteacher from Buena Vista, Georgia, got his first Plott hound from his great-uncle Robert Jones at the age of twelve. He began coon hunting with Jones and their Plott dogs when he was fifteen. John was bitten hard by the "Plott bug," and though he tried other dogs as he grew older, he always came back to the Plotts.

John Hagin on left with his buckskin-colored Plott hound Bentley and James McQue of the ABAC Cooners Club. Hagin started the first officially sanctioned collegiate hunting hound club in the United States and is the great-nephew of Plott hound legend Robert Jones.

By the time Hagin entered college at Abraham Baldwin Agricultural College, or ABAC, in Tipton, Georgia, he was an experienced coon hunter and Plott dog man. He was surprised to learn that many of his classmates shared his interest in coon hunting with Plotts. In the autumn of 2002, Hagin and his friends decided to start their own collegiate coon hunting club. They soon made their presentation to both the dean of student affairs, as well as the student body of ABAC (a satellite school of the Universtiy of Georgia), and it was quickly approved.

By the spring of 2003, the club known as the ABAC Cooners had also become an officially registered UKC chartered club. The club had their first registered hunt that year with twenty-five members and their dogs entered. John Hagin graduated from the University of Georgia in 2005 and is now a high school teacher in Thomaston, Georgia. Yet his legacy lives on with the ABAC Cooners. The club now has seventy-five members, male and female, and remains the first and only collegiate club of its kind in the United States. Thanks in part to John Hagin and other like-minded youngsters, the popularity of the Plott hound breed remains stronger than ever in 2007.

The AKC, the world's largest dog registry, registered more than four hundred Plott pups in 2006. And the UKC—which does not publicly release these figures—probably registered twice that many or more. Plus, these numbers do not take into account the literally thousands of Plott pups that were not formally registered. Though long recognized as an official breed by both clubs, the Plott hound was not granted formal recognition as a show dog in the hound category by the AKC until January 1, 2007. That same month, a beautiful Plott hound owned by breeder, owner and handler Christina Farthing graced the cover of the monthly AKC publication, the *AKC Gazette*, along with a feature article by Maria Bovsun.

These events opened an entirely new chapter for the Plott hound breed as a show dog. Now the Plott hound could compete with the most prestigious purebred dogs in the world at events like the illustrious Westminster Abbey Dog Show, as well as other AKC-sanctioned dog shows. Many grizzled, veteran Plott hound bear hunters frown upon this, saying that the true measure of the Plott dog is in the woods—not a show stage. And that is true—at least in terms of what the dog was originally intended for. Still, this type of exposure in my opinion can do nothing but help promote the breed.

Amanda Alexander of Homer City, Pennsylvania, a master groomer, trainer, hunter and kennel owner, owns the first Plott hound to be finished to champion in AKC conformation show events. Alexander's dog, a Plott hound named Black Monday, won the crown early in 2007. The previously mentioned Christina Farthing, a renowned trainer in bench competitions, now plans to campaign two of her Plotts, County Line Krueger and County Line Liberty Bell, in AKC show events. (See definition of bench and conformation events in the Glossary.)

Though this is yet another challenge for the Plott hound, it is one that should pose no problem for them. After centuries of battling big game in the wilderness, the breed won't have a problem adapting to a big city dog show. As Amanda Alexander said about her Plott hounds in the January 2007 *AKC Gazette*: "They are fearless. Things don't bother them. Going to a dog show should be just another day for a Plott."

In that same article, the author notes how some Plotts have been trained in Texas for obedience competitions. Bovsun also reports that two Plott hounds owned by Sonia Yearwood—Skyplott Sunstreak and Skyplott Teddy Bear—have both won titles in the sport. Yearwood is quoted as saying that the Plotts "are just a highly intelligent and trainable dog." Even the tough old icons of the Big Five would have to agree with that.

Dog trainer Linda Williams has successfully trained a Plott hound to work as a search and rescue dog. Now Plott hounds are routinely used nationwide as tracking dogs looking for criminals or those lost in the wild. Lester Munday of Trinidad, Colorado, has hunted mountain lions with his Plotts for almost thirty years. Last year he and his dogs helped Colorado wildlife officials in a study of the big cats and tagged nine mountain lions in the process.

I find it interesting that Plott hound enthusiasts of today are describing their Plott hounds in a manner very similar to the legends of the golden age and old-time era— using terms like fearless, intelligent and highly trainable. Sounds familiar doesn't it?

The 2007 Plott hound is a respected big game dog, coonhound, show dog, search and rescue dog, field trial competitor, an official state dog and a great family pet. The breed is recognized by all major kennel clubs and supported by two national organizations devoted specifically to the animal. The twenty-first-century Plott hound can do it all and do it well. It is somewhat ironic, yet somehow fitting, that the old-time multipurpose Plott hound has now become a modern-day multipurpose dog. Certainly their various talents today differ from those of the old-time dogs. Their risks today are fewer, and their duties, for the most part, are vastly different. Most of them aren't in the woods or on the farm every day like the fabled old-time dogs of the past. Nor are their owners dependent on them for their survival. But make no mistake about it, they are still in their own way multipurpose dogs. And good ones.

Many traditionalists (and I consider myself a traditionalist) may scoff at this comparison. But I believe it to be a valid one. Why? Because despite the best efforts of some breeders and individuals who have sold Plott dogs just for the money, and who care nothing for lineage or tradition, the Plott hound has continued to thrive for almost three centuries as a multipurpose dog. But most of all, I think it is because of the wide range of people who are fiercely devoted to the preservation and perpetuation of the breed. People of all ages, races, professions and genders are united in their passion and love for the Plott hound, and they have proven their commitment to the dog.

Whatever the circumstances surrounding his reasons for first bringing his dogs to America, Johannes Plott surely loved his Plott hounds. And he instilled that love into his family and their friends and supporters, so deeply in fact, that the Plott hound still reigns supreme today as the premier hunting and multipurpose dog in America, perhaps the world.

The Plott hounds of today love what they do, just as they always have. It is in the core of their very being—the Plott hound was, and is, first and foremost, a hunting dog. They love their owners and they love to hunt, just as their owners love them and their sport. It is a love as big as the great outdoors, and it has to be to still burn so brightly today. The story of the Plott hound, and indeed the family itself, is uniquely different from

Above: Bob Plott with Crockett's Archie, a Purple Ribbon, UKC-registered Crockett-Plott with strong bloodlines from Taylor Crockett, Lawrence Porterfield and Isaiah Kidd.

Below: Jacob Plott, great-great-great-great-grandson of Johannes Plott, with his pup Plott's Bud, a seventh-generation Von Plott dog bred by C.E. "Bud" Lyon.

any other. From the German origins of the hound, to its journey to, and refinement in, America, it is a story that is "pure Americana," as John Jackson best put it.

Never in his wildest dreams could Johannes Plott have imagined that the five dogs he brought to America would ever have gained such wide-ranging popularity. But as Von Plott said in Chapter Two, Johannes certainly had the foresight to know the value of what he had and the importance of preserving it and improving it. And for that we are forever in his debt.

While he may never have envisioned the fame of his family or dogs, I am sure my great-great-great-grandfather Johannes (George) Plott would be proud of them both. I know that I am. And I know that I want to do my small part in preserving and protecting what he so wisely and bravely began almost three hundred years ago. But regardless of what my minor role or that of any of my relatives may be, the legacy of our family and dogs is safe and will endure forever, due to the strength and perseverance of so many dedicated "Plott people" from the past, present and future. Thanks to all of them for keeping our dream alive.

METHVEN BIG GAME AWARD WINNERS

The Methven Big Game Award is the oldest award annually presented pertaining to the Plott hound breed. Frank Methven named the award in memory of his father, grandfathers and uncle. The award is presented yearly by the NPHA, and the list of winners reads like a Plott hound history hall of fame. Many are included in this book. The winners from 1955 to 1958 were presented posthumously. The winners from 1955 to 2006 were:

1955	Johannes Plott
1956	Henry Plott
1957	John Plott
1958	Montraville Plott
1959	John A. Plott
1960	Gola P. Ferguson
1961	Isaiah Kidd
1962	Taylor Crockett
1963	H.V. "Von" Plott
1964	Samuel Plott
1965	"Hack" Smithdeal
1966	"Rags" Nichols
1967	Dale Brandenburger
1968	Colonel Bennie Moore
1969	Herbert Plott
1970	Kermit Allison
1971	Everette Weems
1972	C.E. "Bud" Lyon
1973	Leroy Haug
1974	Ray Jones
1975	Ron Hills

1976   Carl Roark
1977   Bill Bland
1978   Steve Mohr
1979   Dwayne and Steve Herd (father and son)
1980   Frank Staab
1981   Willis Butolph
1982   Tom Telford
1983   Duane Smith
1984   Berlin King
1985   Leo Dollins
1986   Andrew Blankenship
1987   Elmer Allen
1988   Ernst and Jim Polly (father and son)
1989   Larry McKenzie
1990   Ray and Kenny Jones (father and son)
1991   Clyde Bounds
1992   William "Bill" Plott
1993   Luis Fred Albiser
1994   Gene White
1995   Reverend Robert Whitehead
1996   Eugene Walker
1997   A.L. "Cheyenne" Hill
1998   Curtis Walker
1999   Ellet Bias
2000   John Banks
2001   Charles Gantte
2002   James R. Brown
2003   Rex Meinert
2004   Wayne Allen
2005   Roy Stiles
2006   John Jackson

The National Plott Hound Association has a fine website—www.mynpha.com—that provides a lot of valuable information about both their organization and the Plott hound breed. In addition to the Methven Award winners they have several other awards dating from 1965 to 2005 that pertain to the top Plott dogs, breeders, hunters and owners from that time period. There are more than one hundred winners listed here. I highly recommend it.

Glossary of Terms

There are literally hundreds, perhaps thousands, of terms used by Plott hound owners, hunters and breeders to describe the skills and traits of their dogs. These terms sometimes vary geographically, and often there is disagreement as to their use and definition. For example, some experts feel that the term "strike and stay" is a term best used for running dogs such as foxhounds, rather than for tree dogs like Plotts. Yet almost every Plott hound person I spoke with repeatedly used the terms strike and stay to compliment their Plott hounds. Meaning, of course, that their best dogs would strike a trail and stay on it, or stay in the fight until it was done, no matter what the cost.

Here are a few of the more commonly used terms, or references, as well as some organizations often associated with the Plott hound breed:

American Kennel Club or AKC: One of the two most prestigious and largest purebred dog registries in the United States—the other being the United Kennel Club. Formed in 1884, the AKC is the oldest American kennel club, and it recognizes the buckskin-colored Plott, while the UKC does not.

American Plott Association or APA: Club founded in 1987 to promote the Plott hound and preserve the buckskin Plott. The APA is the national organization designated by the AKC to represent the Plott hound.

babbler: A hound that barks or bays when not on a game trail or bay tree.

bawl mouth: A term used to describe a hound's bark. The bawl mouth hound barks with a long, drawn-out voice, usually deep, or bass, in texture. Plott hounds typically bawl on cold tracks and chop as the trail warms up. A bawl mouth is appreciated by many pleasure hunters for its value and is generally regarded by hunters to be the most beautiful of all hound voices. It is important to note, however, that while Plott dogs bark both ways, most hounds tend to be classified as one or the other—a chop-mouthed or bawl-mouthed dog. And some hunters or owners value one more than the other based on personal preference.

bay: The prolonged voice or bark of a hunting hound. Can also apply to having game contained or "bayed" on the ground, or at the game or bay tree.

bay dog: Term used in bear hunting to describe the dogs that bay or contain the bear while treed or on the ground. The bay dog is generally more aggressive and not as good a tracker or as cold-nosed as the strike dog.

bench show: A competition generally held at hound-oriented field events. It is similar to a conformation show. At bench shows the dogs are judged from both the bench (or table) and the ground on their overall appearance and adherence to breed standards. In bench shows, the Plott hound's handler will attempt to "stack" their dog to best display their attributes.

black saddle: Also known simply as a saddleback. A term used to describe the solid black color from the base of the neck to the hip of the hound, which resembles a saddle. The Blevins-Plott hounds were well known for this characteristic, though it is shared by other Plott hounds too. This trait almost always occurs when a high tan and brindle Plott are bred together.

blue merle: A color pattern of dark or black splotches on a blue/gray background.

booger barker: A dog that barks and remains a safe or comfortable distance from their prey, rather than more agressively pursuing it.

breed standard: The officially sanctioned description of the ideal or perfect example of a specific dog breed.

brindle: A term that refers to the coat color of the dog. Brindle coloring indicates a striping over a lighter or darker base color, with shades varying from yellow, tan, red or brown, to almost black. Plott dogs are world renowned for their various shades of brindle coloring.

brood bitch: A female dog (bitch) used specifically for breeding.

catch dog: A term used mostly in hog hunting to describe a more aggressive hound used to fight and catch or bay game. In hog hunting, the catch dog literally does just that: it bites and catches or holds onto the hog's leg or ear. The catch dog is usually not as good a trailing canine as a strike dog, and it is usually released to follow the strike dog once it has established the game trail. In western states many Plott hound owners use the term "cut" dog to describe a catch dog.

chop mouth: Another term used to describe a Plott hound's bark. The chop mouth hound barks with a sharp staccato, or quick cadence resembling the sound of an axe chopping wood. The chop mouth hound is generally perceived to be faster on the track, or trail, than a bawl mouth dog. Most hounds bawl mouth bark while trailing and chop mouth bark when their prey is treed or bayed. Some Plott experts feel that the old-time Plott hound was strictly a solid chop mouth dog.

cold-nosed: Term used to describe the trailing abilities of a hound. The cold-nosed dog has the capability to "strike" (or find) older, colder trails. Some of these trails could be hours, or even days old, yet the cold-nosed hound has the ability to often find it.

conformation: A term used to describe how well a dog conforms to their established breed standard. See UKC and AKC Plott hound breed standards in Chapter 9 and Chapter 11.

conformation show: Competition determined by judges based on how well the dog adheres to established breed standards.

cry: The baying, barking or "music" of a hound on a game trail.

dam: Term used to describe the mother of a pup.

date of whelping: Pup's date of birth.

double coat: An outer, protective, weather- and brush-resistant coat of hair, combined with a water-resistant, warm undercoat. This trait is found sometimes, but is not common in Plotts.

drag: Laying a trail with a game scent for field competitions.

field trial: A simulated hunting competition whereby a scent trail is laid across varied terrain, ending at a home tree containing either a caged raccoon or a raccoon-scented lure. The starting line must not be visible from the home tree. Dogs are released by the judge at the starting line and they are expected to run the scent trail to the tree. A finish line is indicated by placing stakes near the home tree, through which the dogs must pass. The first dog to cross the finish line is the "line winner," and the first hound to bark up the home tree is the "tree winner." The AKC and UKC both offer field trial champion titles to winning dogs in these events. Field trials may also be held using other animal scents such as bear, bobcat or mountain lion. Plott hounds are eligible for and often win these events in both small and big game categories.

foundation stock: The first generation of an officially registered specific dog breed.

gestation period: Time between date of conception and birth, usually about sixty-five days for Plotts.

get deep quick: Refers to a hound that has the ability to quickly cover a large area in order to strike a game trail.

going deep: Refers to a dog that will go as far as necessary to find a game trail. Sometimes also described as "hunting wide."

Grand Nite Champion: Dog that has won the required specified number of titles at nite hunt events. See nite hunt.

gun dog: A dog trained to find and pursue game.

gyp: Term used to describe a female dog.

hot-nosed: Another term used to describe the trailing abilities of a hound. The hot-nosed hound is better on very "hot," very fresh or more recent game trail.

inbreeding: A term used to describe breeding dogs very closely within their own family. In most cases this refers to the breeding of a mother or father to their pup or brother to sister.

in whelp: Term used to describe a pregnant dog.

kennel name: The officially registered or protected name of a dog, usually indicating where it originated. The Plott family, for example, registered most of their dogs using "Plott's" as the prefix for the animal's name, such as Plott's Belle. Others use the term to clearly identify their kennel or strain such as Haug's Swampland strain of Plotts, or the Fielder's Bear Pen Plotts.

lead: A leash, rope, chain or cord that hunters or handlers attach to their Plott's collar. Used to restrain or lead the hound.

linebreeding: Another term used to describe the breeding of dogs within their own family, but in this case a bit further apart, such as uncle to niece, aunt to nephew or cousin, etc. Dog breeders use these methods—especially linebreeding—to gather as many genes as possible of a specific dog. By breeding back to the canine whose traits they hope to reproduce, they at least produce dogs with similar traits.

maltese: Also called blue, the term is used to describe some grayish blue–colored Plott hounds. The maltese color factor is the result of dilution, whereby the color gene that normally produces black is diluted. Von Plott's Blueboy was a notable maltese-colored Plott hound.

merle: Another color term used to describe the marbled or spotted colors on a white, tan or dark background. Sometimes also referred to as a leopard-colored dog, such as the leopard Plotts, though usually associated with other breeds, such as sheepdogs, leopard curs and Catahoulas.

mutation: Sudden change in a bloodline that is drastically different than their immediate forebears.

National Plott Hound Association or NPHA: Club founded in 1954 to better promote and advance the Plott hound breed. The NPHA is the national organization designated by the UKC to represent the Plott breed. Neither the NPHA nor the UKC officially recognize the buckskin-colored Plott hound.

nite or night hunt: An event usually sanctioned by one or both of the major kennel clubs specifically for coonhounds. It is similar to a field trial, except in this case the dogs are drawn by lottery into groups of four and enter the woods in these groups to compete for a title. Once in the woods, the hounds are expected to hunt and tree raccoons in their native habitat. A point system based on the dogs' abilities to strike and tree is used to score the competition. The winning hound at the end of the competition, called a cast, is known as the cast winner. In the AKC, five cast wins earns the title AKC Nite Champion. Advanced titles such as Grand Nite Champion and Supreme Nite Champion can also be won. No guns are involved and no animals are killed in these contests. Plott hounds have done exceptionally well in these events.

outcrossing: The mating of unrelated dogs of the same specific pure breed.

pack: Several hounds kept together at one location or kennel. A mixed pack indicates that both males and females are in the pack.

pack dog: A dog generally released after the strike dog establishes the trail. These dogs then "pack" the trail to increase pressure on the game and provide more "dog power" to the chase.

pedigree: A documented record of a dog's genealogy dating back at least three generations.

proven producer: A stud Plott hound that has the proven ability to sire high-quality pups from a variety of different females or dams.

purebred: A Plott dog whose sire and dam are of unmixed descent since official recognition of the breed.

registered name: The name a dog is given by its owner or buyer, which is assigned to it when its paperwork is processed.

saber tail: Tail carried in a high semicircle, a breed standard for Plotts.

scent hound: Dog that runs courses or game by scent rather than sight. A sight hound is just the opposite and runs game by sight rather than scent.

scissors bite: The preferred standard bite for a Plott, where the outer side of the lower incisors touches the inner side of the upper incisors.

sight hound: Dog that trails by sight rather than scent, generally a more hot-nosed dog.

single tracking: Ideal standard for a Plott hound's gait at full speed. Indicates that all footprints are falling on a single line of travel. The greater the speed, the closer the paws come to tracking on a single line.

sire: Term used to describe a father of a pup, also known as a stud dog.

strike dog: A more cold-nosed hound with superior trailing skills used to strike (or establish) a definite game trail for the rest of the pack to follow.

stud dog: Male hound used for breeding purposes. Often a fee is charged for stud service of Plotts with a well-established lineage.

tongue: Word or term sometimes used to describe hounds barking or baying on the game trail.

tracking collar: Electronic collar used by hunters to locate or track their Plott hounds while hunting.

trail: To hunt or track game by following ground scent of the desired game.

United Kennel Club or UKC: One of the two largest, and second oldest, purebred dog registries in the United States. The UKC was established in 1898 and is affiliated with the NPHA. The UKC does not recognize the buckskin-colored Plott as an acceptable standard color.

whelped or whelping: Term used to describe the delivery of pups, such as "Plott's June (a pup) was whelped by Plott's Flirt (the pup's mother)."

wind: To catch a game scent.

withers: Highest point of a dog's shoulders.

BIBLIOGRAPHY

BOOKS AND MEDIA

Allen, W.C. *History of Haywood County*. Waynesville, NC: Haywood County Historical Society, 1935.

American Plott Association 2003 Yearbook. Printed by the APA, 2003.

American Plott Association 2004 Yearbook. Printed by the APA, 2004.

American Plott Association 2005 Yearbook. Printed by the APA, 2005.

American Plott Association 2006 Yearbook. Printed by the APA, 2006.

Arnow, Harriette Simpson. *Seedtime on the Cumberland*. Louisville: University Press of Kentucky, 1983.

Bovsun, Maria. "True Grit." *The AKC Gazette Magazine*. January 2007.

Camp, Raymond. "Dog Stalks Bear for 74 Hours." *New York Times*. December 11, 1947.

Coggins, Allen R. *Place Names of the Smokies*. Gatlinburg, TN: Great Smoky Mountains Natural History Association, 1999.

Duffy, Kevin. *Who Were the Celts?* New York: Barnes and Noble Publishing, 1999.

Earley, Lawrence, and Wooten Curtis. "Taylor Crockett Remembers." *Wildlife In North Carolina*. February 1985.

Ellison, Elizabeth, and George Ellison. *Blue Ridge Nature Journal*. Charleston, SC: The History Press, 2006.

Ellison, George. "Mark Cathey." In *The Heritage of Swain County, North Carolina*. Edited by Hazel C. Jenkins. Winston Salem, NC: History Division of Hunter Publishing, 1988.

————. *Mountain Passages: Natural and Cultural History of Western North Carolina and the Great Smoky Mountains*. Charleston, SC: The History Press, 2005.

Frome, Michael. *Strangers in High Places*. Knoxville: University of Tennessee Press, 1966.

Gasque, Jim. *Hunting and Fishing in the Great Smokies*. New York: Alfred A. Knopf, 1947.

Hunnicutt, Samuel J. *Twenty Years of Hunting and Fishing in the Great Smoky Mountains*. Knoxville, TN: S.B. Newman, 1926.

Kephart, Horace. "Bear Hunt in the Smokies." *Forest and Stream*. October 28, 1905.

————. *Our Southern Highlanders: A Narrative of Adventure in the Southern Appalachians and a Study of Life Among the Mountaineers*. Reprinted with an introduction by George Ellison. Knoxville: University of Tennessee Press, 1976.

Methven, Frank T. *The Sound of Hills*. Pittsburgh, PA: Dorrance Publishing Company Inc., 2006.

National Plott Hound Association 1968 Yearbook. Printed by the NPHA, 1968.

National Plott Hound Association 1970 Yearbook. Printed by the NPHA, 1970.

National Plott Hound Association 1979 Yearbook. Printed by the NPHA, 1979.

Neufeld, Rob. *A Popular History of Western North Carolina: Mountains, Heroes and Hootnoggers*. Charleston, SC: The History Press, 2007.

Oney, Steve. "The Wilderness Campaign." *Atlanta Journal Constitution Magazine*. September 24, 1978.

Parris, John. *Mountain Bred*. Asheville, NC: Citizen Times Publishing Company, 1967.

————. *Roaming The Mountains*. Asheville, NC: Citizen Times Publishing Company, 1955.

————. *These Storied Mountains*. Asheville, NC: Citizen Times Publishing Company, 1972.

Pennsylvania Gazette. May 1, 1760.

Pitard, Janet. "The State Dog." *Our State Magazine.* October 2006.

Powell, William S. *The Encyclopedia of North Carolina.* Chapel Hill: University of North Carolina Press, 2006.

————. *The North Carolina Gazetteer: A Dictionary of Tar Heel Places.* Chapel Hill: University of North Carolina Press, 1968.

Robinson, Jerome B. "The Most Prized Big Game Dog In The World." *Sports Afield.* April 1973.

Rupp, Israel Daniel. *A Collection of Upwards of 30,000 Names of German, Swiss, Dutch, and French in Pennsylvania from 1727–1776.* Philadelphia: Genealogical Publishing Company, 1876.

Spangenburg, Augustus Gottlieb. *The Spangenberg Diary.* Records of the Moravians in North Carolina, edited by Adelaide L. Fries, 1. Raleigh: North Carolina Historical Association, 1922.

Strutin, Michael. *History Hikes of the Great Smokies.* Gatlinburg, TN: Great Smoky Mountains Natural History Association, 2003.

"Top Ten Plott Stud Dogs of All Time." *UKC Bloodlines Magazine.* July 2000.

Verhoef, Esther. *The Complete Encyclopedia of Dogs.* Edison, NJ: Chartwell Books, 2001.

Whitney, Leon. *The Basis of Dog Breeding.* E.C. Fowler, 1928.

————. *How to Breed Dogs.* Orange Judd, 1962.

Wigginton, Elliott. *Foxfire Five.* Garden City, NY: Anchor Press/Doubleday, 1979.

Wooten, Curtis. "Johannes Plott's Famous Hunting Dogs." *Wildlife in North Carolina.* October 1983.

Zeigler, Wilbur G., and Ben S. Grosscup. *The Heart of the Alleghenies or Western North Carolina: Comprising Its Topography, History, Resource, People, Narratives, Incidents, and Pictures of Travel. Adventures in Hunting and Fishing and Legends of Its Wilderness.* Raleigh, NC: Alfred Williams and Company, 1883.

Bibliography

Websites

American Kennel Club–www.akc.org
Blackmouth Cur–www.blackmouthcur.com
Breeds of Dogs–www.thebreedsofdogs.com
Canine Breeds–http://caninebreeds.com
Dog Breed Information–www.dogbreedinfo.com
Furry Critters–www.furrycritter.com
National Plott Hound Association–www.mynpha.org
Pets (dogs)–www.petplace.com
Plott Hounds–www.Plottdogs.com
United Kennel Club–www.ukcdog.com
Wikipedia (English)–http://en.wikipedia.org
Wikipedia (German)–http://ger.wikipedia.org

About the Author

R obert "Bob" Plott is a great-great-great-grandson of Johannes Plott. He has spent most of his professional career working either as a manufacturing manager or as a martial arts instructor. He is an avid outdoorsman and an accomplished woodcarver and sketch artist. Bob is a member of the American Plott Association, the National Plott Hound Association and the North Carolina Bear Hunters Association. This, his first book, is the 2008 winner of the Willie Parker Peace Award, which is given annually to the best North Carolina historical book. He lives with his wife, son and their Plott hounds outside of Statesville, North Carolina.

Author photo by Kaitlyn O'Neil Talbert.

Visit us at
www.historypress.net